International English Language Testing System

IELTS™

English for International Opportunity

English - Persian

It is important to have a flexible use of a wide range of vocabulary for IELTS as the examiner will be looking for this in the writing and speaking. It is also necessary for your reading so that you understand the texts as they will have a lot of difficult words.

abandonment (رها کردن) giving up completely, freedom from constraint	**abbreviation** (مخفف) shortening something by omitting parts of it
abeyance (اطاعت) suspended action, temporary cessation or suspension	**abnormal** (غیر طبیعی) unusual, not typical, not normal
abolish (لغو) cancel, put an end to, destroy completely	**abolition** (لغو) ending, act of abolishing, act of doing away with
abortive (سقط جنین) unsuccessful, failing to accomplish an intended objective, fruitless	**abrogate** (لغو) abolish, do away with, or annul, especially by authority
absence (غیبت) state of being absent, state of being away	**absent** (غایب) go away or leave , missing, not present
absolute (مطلق) perfect in quality or nature, complete, totally unlimited, certain	**absolutely** (کاملا) utterly, definitely
absorb (جذب) assimilate or incorporate, suck or drink up, occupy full attention	**absurd** (چرند) preposterous, ridiculously incongruous or unreasonable, foolish
abundance (فراوانی) great or plentiful amount, fullness to overflowing	**abundant** (فراوان) plentiful, possessing riches or resources
abuse (سو استفاده کردن) improper use or handling, misuse	**accede** (پیوستن) agree, give consent, often at insistence of another, concede
access (دسترسی) approach, entry, entrance	**accidental** (تصادفی) unexpected, unforeseen

accompaniment (همراهی) act of accompanying someone or something	**accompany** (همراهی کردن) travel with, be associated with
accomplishment (دستاورد) achievement, fulfillment	**accountant** (حسابدار) one who maintains and audits business accounts
accounting (حسابداری) system that provides quantitative information about finances	**accumulate** (انباشتن) pile up, collect, mount up, increase
accumulation (انباشت) increase by natural growth or addition, concentration	**accuracy** (دقت) quality of nearness to the truth or the true value
accuse (متهم کردن) blame, condemn	**achieve** (رسیدن) gain with effort, accomplish, fulfill
acknowledge (اذعان) declare to be true or admit, express obligation, thanks	**acquaint** (آشنا) inform about, cause to come to know personally, make familiar
acquaintance (آشنایی) personal knowledge or information about someone or something	**acquainted** (آشنا) known by or familiar with another, informed or familiar
acquisition (تحصیل) act of contracting or assuming or acquiring possession of something	**across** (در سراسر) from side to side, crosswise, or in a direction opposed to the length
activate (فعال کنید) make active or more active, stimulate, make radioactive	**actual** (واقعی) true, real, being, existing, or acting at the present moment, current
actually (در حقیقت) truly, really, in fact	**adaptation** (انطباق) modification, alteration or adjustment in structure or habits

additional (اضافی) further, extra, supplemental or added to	**adequate** (کافی است) sufficient, enough to meet a purpose
adhere (پایبندی) stick fast, stick to firmly, be compatible or in accordance with	**adhesive** (چسب) glue, paste , substance that unites or bonds surfaces together
adjacent (مجاور) adjoining, neighboring, close to, lying near	**adjoin** (مجاور) be next to, be contiguous to, border on
adjust (تنظیم) adapt, regulate	**adjustment** (تنظیم) making or becoming suitable, adjusting to circumstances
administer (اداره) govern, supervise, give or apply medications	**administrative** (اداری) of or relating to or responsible for administration
admiration (تحسین) favorable judgment, feeling of pleasure, wonder, and approval	**admission** (پذیرش) act or practice of admitting, power or permission to enter
admittedly (مسلماً) doubtlessly, in an acknowledged manner, confessedly	**adolescent** (بزرگسالی) a juvenile between the onset of puberty and maturity,
adopt (اتحاذ کردن) accept, take on, raise, take into one's family	**adult** (بالغ) one who has attained maturity or legal age, fully grown
advance (پیشرفت) proceed, move forward, improve, moving forward	**advanced** (پیشرفته) improved, highly developed or complex, ahead of the times, progressive
adventure (ماجرا) something happens without design, chance, hazard, risk, danger	**adversary** (دشمن) opponent in contest, someone who offers opposition

adversity
(سختی)
state of misfortune, hardship, or affliction, misfortune

advertise
(تبلیغات)
give notice to, inform or apprise, make known, give public notice of

advocate
(مدافع)
speak, plead, or argue in favour of, plead for, push for something

affect
(تاثیر می‌گذارد)
have an emotional or cognitive impact upon

affection
(محبت)
fondness, tender feeling toward another, fondness

affiliate
(وابسته)
associate, incorporate

affirm
(تصدیق کنید)
assert, confirm

affirmative
(مثبت)
confirmative, ratifying, giving assent or approval, confirming

agent
(عامل)
one that acts on behalf of other persons or organizations

aggregate
(تجمیع)
gather into a mass, sum, or whole, amount to

aggregation
(تجمع)
several things grouped together or considered as a whole

aggressor
(متجاوز)
one that engages in aggression, person who first attacks

agitate
(تحریک کردن)
cause to move with violence or sudden force, upset, disturb

agitation
(تحریک)
anxiety, extreme emotional disturbance

agreeable
(قابل قبول)
ready to consent or submit, acceptable

agreement
(توافق)
state of agreeing, harmony of opinion, statement, action, or character

agriculture
(کشاورزی)
practice of cultivating the land or raising stock

ailment
(ناراحتی)
sickness, illness, affliction

air
(هوا)
be broadcast on television or radio

alignment
(هم‌ترازی)
arrangement, association, alliance

alike (به طور یکسان) similar, in the same manner or to the same degree	**allergic** (حساسیتی) excessively sensitive, susceptible, having an allergy
allocate (اختصاص دادن) assign, distribute according to plan	**allowance** (کمک هزینه) approval, act of allowing, granting, or admitting
alloy (آلیاژ) combine, mix, make less pure, lessen or moderate	**ally** (متحد) confederate, partner, collaborator
alone (تنها) solitary, by oneself	**alongside** (در کنار) along or by the side, side by side with
alter (تغییر دهید) modify, cause to change, make different, convert	**alternation** (متناوب) successive change from one thing or state to another and back again
aluminum (آلومینیوم) silvery ductile metallic element	**amateur** (آماتور) nonprofessional, lacking the skill of a professional, as in an art
amazement (حیرت) wonder, state of extreme surprise or wonder, astonishment	**ambassador** (سفیر) authorized messenger or representative
ambiguity (گنگ) state of being ambiguous, doubtfulness or uncertainty	**ambiguous** (مبهم) unclear or doubtful in meaning
ambitious (بلند پروازانه) aspiring, having a strong desire for success or achievement	**amend** (اصلاح) change for the better, improve, remove faults or errors
amendment (اصالحیه) correction, revision	**amends** (اصلاح می کند) compensation for a loss or injury, recompense, reparation

amiable
(دوستانه)
good-natured and likable, lovable, warmly friendly

amicable
(دوستانه)
exhibiting friendliness or goodwill, not quarrelsome

amid
(در میان)
in the middle of, among, surrounded by

amount
(میزان)
total of two or more quantities, aggregate, sum

ample
(کافی)
more than enough in size or scope or capacity, fairly large

amplification
(تَقویت)
addition of extra material or illustration or clarifying detail

analogy
(تَقلید)
similarity in some respects, comparison based on similarity

analytical
(تحلیلی)
of analysis, resolving into elements or parts

analyze
(تجزیه و تحلیل)
diagnose, examine

ancestor
(اجداد)
forefather, forebear, forerunner or predecessor

anchor
(لنگر)
secure or fasten firmly, be fixed in place, narrate or coordinate

angular
(زاویه ای)
sharp-cornered, consisting of an angle or angles, stiff in manner

animate
(تحریک کردن)
endowed with life, alive, living, animated

ankle
(مچ پا)
joint which connects the foot with the leg, tarsus

announce
(اعلام)
herald, give out, proclaim, make known publicly

announcement
(اعلام)
formal public statement, act of making known publicly

announcer
(گوینده)
one who proclaims a message publicly

annoy
(اذیت کردن)
disturb, especially by minor irritations, irritate

annual
(سالانه)
occurring or payable every year

annually
(سالانه)
yearly, each year, returning every year, year by year

anticipate (پیش بینی) act in advance of, deal with ahead of time, predict	**anticipation** (پیش بینی) something expected, pleasurable expectation, wishing with confidence
antique (عتیقه) any furniture old and valuable, out of fashion	**anyhow** (در هر صورت) in any way or manner whatever, at any rate, in any event
ape (بوزینه) imitate, mimic, as an ape imitates human actions	**apologize** (عذر خواهی کردن) beg pardon
appeal (درخواست) attraction, charm, attract, fascinate, challenge	**appealing** (جذاب) attractive, charming
appendix (ضمیمه) something appended or added	**appetite** (اشتها، میل) instinctive physical desire, especially one for food or drink
apply (درخواست دادن) exert, put into service, avail oneself to,	**appoint** (منصوب کردن) designate, nominate
appreciable (قابل تقدیر) considerable, perceptible	**appreciate** (قدردانی) be thankful for, increase in worth, be thoroughly conscious of
appreciation (قدردانی) recognition, taste, judgment or opinion, especially a favorable one	**appreciative** (قدردانی) having or showing a just or ready appreciation or perception
apprentice (شاگرد کارآموز) works for an expert to learn a trade, beginner, learner	**approach** (رویکرد) access, method
approval (تصویب) official approbation, endorsement, act of approving	**approve** (تایید) ratify, consider right or good, think or speak favorably of

approximate
(تَقریبی)

approach, come near

apt
(مناسب)

likely, exactly suitable, appropriate, quick to learn or understand

arc
(قوس)

continuous portion of a circle, something curved in shape

arch
(قوس)

any part of a curved line

archaeology
(باستان شناسی)

study of artifacts and relics of early mankind

ardent
(سرسخت)

displaying or by strong enthusiasm or devotion, passionate

arduous
(دشوار)

demanding great effort or labor, difficult

aristocracy
(اشرافیت)

hereditary nobility, privileged class

arithmetic
(حساب)

theory of numerical calculations

arms
(بازوها)

weapons considered collectively, official symbols of a family

arouse
(برانگیختن)

excite, stimulate, awaken from or as if from sleep

arrangement
(آرایش)

composition, order

array
(آرایه)

set out for display or use, place in orderly arrangement

arrest
(دستگیری)

stop or slow down, catch someone's attention, take into custody

article
(مقاله)

essay, editorial, individual thing or element of a class

artificial
(ساختگی)

made by humans, produced rather than natural.

ascertain
(مشخص)

find out for certain, discover with certainty, make sure of

ashamed
(شرمنده)

affected by shame, abashed or confused by guilt

assault
(حمله)

attack, onslaught

assemble
(جمع کردن)

put together, bring or call together into a group or whole

assert
(ادعا)
declare or state with confidence, put oneself forward boldly

assess
(ارزیابی)
estimate value, judge worth of something

assign
(اختصاص دادن)
appoint, allot, make over, point out authoritatively or exactly

assignment
(وظیفه)
task given to students, job, distribution, appointment

assist
(کمک)
give help or support to, especially as a subordinate

assistant
(دستیار)
helper, person who assists or helps someone else

associate
(وابسته)
connect or join together, combine

assorted
(متنوع)
varied, miscellaneous

assume
(فرض)
suppose, presume, take on, bear

assurance
(اطمینان)
promise or pledge, certainty, self-confidence, freedom from doubt

assure
(اطمینان دادن)
solidify, guarantee, convince

assured
(حاضر جمع)
made sure, exhibiting confidence or authority, indubitable

astronomer
(ستاره شناس)
a physicist who studies astronomy

athlete
(ورزشکار)
sports man, one who contended for prize in public games

atlas
(نقشه اطلس)
a bound volume of maps, charts, or tables

atomic
(اتمی)
of or relating to or comprising atoms, immeasurably small

attach
(ضمیمه کردن)
fasten, annex, be in contact with

attack
(حمله)
offensive move, expression of strong criticism, hostile comment

attain
(دستیابی به)
achieve or accomplish, gain

attempt
(تلاش)
action of trying at something

attendance (حضور) act of being present	**attendant** (شرکت کننده) aide, servant, accompanying, person who participates in a meeting
attentive (توجه) alert and watchful, considerate, thoughtful	**attitude** (نگرش) posture, action, or disposition of a figure or a statue
attraction (جاذبه) appeal, a characteristic that provides pleasure and attracts	**attribute** (صفت) essential quality, reputation, honor
auction (حراج) public sale of property to the highest bidder	**audience** (حضار) a group of people within hearing, crowd seeing a stage performance
auditorium (سالن اجتماعات) area of theater or concert hall where audience sits	**authorize** (اجازه) empower, give permission for, sanction
autobiography (زندگی نامه) biography or story written by yourself	**automate** (خودکار کردن) replace or enhance human labor with machines
automobile (خودرو) self-propelled vehicle suitable for use on street or roadway	**avail** (فایده) turn to advantage of, be of service to, profit, promote
available (در دسترس) convenient for use or disposal, not busy, free, obtainable, accessible	**avenge** (انتقام) take vengeance for something, or on behalf of someone
average (میانگین) typical, mean, achieve or reach on average	**aviation** (هواپیمایی) art or science of flying, flight, aeronautics
avoid (اجتناب کردن) shield away from, prevent	**awful** (خیلی بد و ناخوشایند) causing fear, dread, or terror, extremely bad or unpleasant, terrible

axis
(محور)

the center around which something rotates, pivot

backbone
(ستون فقَرات)

support, mainstay, vertebrate spine or spinal column

bacterium
(باکتری)

single celled organism with no nucleus

badge
(نشان)

distinctive mark, token, or sign worn on the person

baffle
(مشاجره)

frustrate as by confusing or perplexing, impede force or movement of

bait
(طعمه)

harass, tease, lure, entice, or entrap

balance
(تعادل)

being in equilibrium, equilibrium, symmetry, stability

balcony
(بالکن)

platform projecting from the wall of a building

bald
(بدون مو)

hairless, lacking a natural or usual covering

ballet
(باله)

a sort of theatrical representation by dancers

balloon
(بادکنک)

large non-rigid bag filled with gas or heated air

band
(باند)

orchestra, team, strip, ribbon, belt, unite, ally

bandage
(بانداژ)

strip of woven material, used in dressing and binding up wounds

bang
(انفجار)

a vigorous blow, a conspicuous success

bankrupt
(ورشکسته)

penniless, without any money, financially ruined

banner
(بنر)

flag, sign, a newspaper headline that runs across the full page

banquet
(ضیافت)

feast, entertainment of eating and drinking

bar
(بار)

a counter where you can obtain food or drink, cafe, strip, stick

bare
(لخت)

lacking the usual or appropriate covering or clothing

barely
(به سختی)

just, only, hardly, scarcely

bargain
(چانه زدن)
agreement between parties concerning the sale of property

bark
(پارس سگ)
sound made by a dog, harsh sound uttered by a dog

barometer
(فشار سنج)
instrument for determining the weight or pressure of the atmosphere

baron
(بارون)
title or degree of nobility

barrel
(بشکه)
vessel, large cylindrical container

barren
(بی ثمر)
desolate, fruitless and unproductive, lacking

barrier
(مانع)
obstacle, structure built to bar passage, boundary or limit

basement
(زیر زمین)
cellar, storage room

basin
(حوضه)
bowl-shaped vessel, usually used for holding food or liquids

batter
(خمیر)
beat with successive blows, beat repeatedly and with violence

beak
(منقار)
nib ,horny projecting mouth of a bird

bean
(لوبیا)
various edible seeds, small oval or roundish seed, berry, nut, or lump

bear
(خرس)
support, sustain, carry, have, yield, give birth, hold up or support

beat
(ضرب و شتم)
whip, strike, defeat, hit repeatedly

beforehand
(از قبل)
in state of anticipation, in advance, by way of preparation

behalf
(از طرف)
represent, advantage, benefit, interest of someone

behave
(رفتار کردن)
perform, conduct oneself in a proper way

behavior
(رفتار ـ اخلاق)
conduct, manner

beloved
(محبوب)
greatly loved, dear to the heart

beneficial
(مفید)
helpful, tending to promote physical well-being

beneficiary (ذينفع) person entitled to benefits or proceeds of an insurance policy or will	**benefit** (سود) advantage, something that aids or promotes well-being , welfare, gain
benevolent (خيرانديش) . generous in providing aid to others, charitable	**bent** (خم شده) determined to do or have
besides (بعلاوه) over and above, separate or distinct from, in addition to, other than	**bestow** (هديه دادن) give as gift, present
beverage (نوشيدنی) liquids for drinking, usually excluding water, refreshment	**bewilder** (مبهوت) lead into perplexity or confusion, perplex with mazes
billion (بيليون) the number that is represented as a one followed by 9 zeros	**biographer** (زندگينامه) one who writes a book about somebody's life
biologist (زيست شناس) scientist who studies living organisms	**bitter** (تلخ) harsh or corrosive in tone, painful, acrid, acrimonious
bitterness (تلخی) sharp and bitter manner	**blacksmith** (آهنگر) one who forges and shapes iron with a hammer and anvil
blame (سرزنش) condemn, rebuke, find fault with, censure	**blank** (جای خالی) of a white or pale color, without color, empty, void
blast (انفجار) explode, burst, gale, very strong gust of wind or air	**blaze** (آتش) brilliant burst of fire, destructive fire, flame
bleach (سفيد کننده) make white or colorless, blanch	**bleed** (خونريزی) emit blood, lose blood, withdraw blood from the body

blend	**bless**
(مخلوط کردن)	(برکت)
combination, mixture, forming uniform mixture	make or pronounce holy, consecrate, make happy
blessing	**blink**
(نعمت)	(چشمک زدن)
praying for divine protection, formal act of giving approval	shut eyes briefly, wink
block	**blot**
(مسدود کردن)	(لکه دار کردن)
hinder, obstruct, indicate broadly without great detail, sketch	spot or stain, as of ink on paper, blur, weak point or failing
blunder	**blunt**
(اشتباه بزرگ)	(صاف)
serious mistake typically caused by ignorance or confusion	having a dull edge or end, not sharp, lacking in feeling, insensitive
blush	**boast**
(سرخ شدن)	(به رخ کشیدن)
become rosy or reddish, turn red, as if in embarrassment or shame	show off oneself, speak of with excessive pride
bodyguard	**bold**
(محافظ شخصی)	(جسورانه)
guard to protect or defend person, lifeguard	brave, daring, intrepid, impudent
bolt	**bond**
(پیچ)	(رابطه، رشته)
dash or dart off, move or jump suddenly	link, connection, uniting force or tie, binding agreement, duty
bookcase	**boom**
(قفسه کتاب)	(رونق)
case with shelves for holding books, especially one with glazed doors	bonanza, prosperity, prosper, expand, flourish
booming	**boost**
(رونق گرفتن)	(تَقویت)
deep and resonant, flourishing, thriving	raise, advance, push or shove upward
bore	**boring**
(منفذ)	(حوصله سر بر)
drill, make a hole in or through, with or as if with a drill	uninteresting and tiresome, dull

bounce
(گزاف‌گویی)

jolt, rebound after having struck an object or a surface

bound
(مقَید)

tied, held, committed, limit, constraint, leap, jump

boundary
(مرز)

dividing line, border, frontier

bourgeois
(بورژوازی)

middle class, selfishly materialistic, dully conventional

bowl
(کاسه)

throw or roll a ball, move quickly and smoothly, especially by rolling

boycott
(تحریم کردن)

refrain from buying or using

brain
(مغز)

organ or seat of intellect, understanding or imagination

brake
(ترمز)

a piece of mechanism for retarding or stopping motion by friction

breach
(رخنه)

breaking of contract or duty

breadth
(وسعت)

measure or dimension from side to side, width, extent

breakthrough
(دستیابی به موفقَیت)

act of overcoming or penetrating an obstacle or restriction

breath
(نفس)

air that is inhaled and exhaled in respiration

breathe
(نفس کشیدن)

respire, inhale and exhale air

breed
(نژاد)

raise, produce offspring, give birth to or hatch, mate

breeze
(نسیم)

light current of air, gentle wind, progress swiftly and effortlessly

brief
(مختصر)

short in time, duration, length, or extent, concise

brighten
(روشن تر)

lighten, cheer, encourage, make or become bright or brighter

brilliance
(درخشش)

cleverness, magnificence

brilliant
(درخشان)

full of light, shining, bright, sharp and clear in tone

brim
(لبه)

brink, edge

brittle
(شکننده)

easily broken, having little elasticity

broaden
(گسترده تر)

widen, grow broad or broader

brochure
(بروشور)

pamphlet, small book usually having paper cover

bronze
(برنز)

an alloy of copper and tin and sometimes other elements

brood
(تولد)

think long and anxiously, be in a state of gloomy, serious thought

brook
(نهر)

creek, stream

brown
(رنگ قهوه ای)

of dark color, of various shades between black and red or yellow

bruise
(کبودی)

injure, as by a blow or collision, contuse, fight with the fists

brutal
(بی رحمانه)

like a brute, savage, cruel, inhuman, merciless

bud
(جوانه)

one that is not yet fully developed, sprout

budget
(بودجه)

estimate, a sum of money allocated for a particular purpose

bug
(حشره)

general name applied to various insects

bulk
(فله)

majority, main part, volume, mass

bump
(دست انداز)

impact as from a collision, lump on the body caused by a blow

bunch
(دسته)

clump, cluster, gathering

bundle
(دسته)

packet, a package of things tied together, a large sum of money

burdensome
(سنگین)

not easily borne, wearing, causing uneasiness or fatigue

bush
(بوته)

place abounding in trees or shrubs, wild forest

butter
(کره)

oily, unctuous substance obtained from cream or milk by churning

butterfly
(پروانه)

insect typically having a slender body with broad colorful wings

buzz (وزوز) confusion of activity and gossip, sound of rapid vibration	**bygone** (گذشت) past, gone by
by-product (محصول جانبی) product made during the manufacture of something else	**cab** (تاکسی) taxi, one-horse vehicle for public hire
cabin (کابین) small room on a ship or boat where people sleep	**cable** (کابل) very strong thick rope made of twisted steel or metal wire
cafe (کافه) coffee house, restaurant where coffee and liquors are served	**calculation** (محاسبه) planning something carefully and intentionally
campus (محوطه دانشگاه) field where the buildings of a university are situated	**canal** (کانال) artificial channel filled with water, tube or duct
cancel (لغو) revoke, call off, omit or delete	**cancellation** (لغو) act of cancelling, calling off some arrangement
candid (صادقانه) straightforward, frank, free from prejudice, impartial	**capability** (قابلیت) quality of being capable, capacity, skill
capable (توانا) having the ability required for a specific task	**capacity** (ظرفیت) mental or physical ability, ability to accommodate
caption (زیرنویس) title, chapter heading, text under illustration	**cardinal** (اصلی) chief, serving as an essential component
careless (بی توجه) negligent, taking insufficient care	**cargo** (محموله) freight carried by a ship, an aircraft, or another vehicle

carrier (حامل) one that carries or conveys, messenger	**carton** (کارتن) pasteboard for paper boxes, pasteboard box
carve (تراشیدن) cut, sculpt	**carving** (کنده کاری) cutting away parts to create a desired shape
cashier (صندوقدار) one who has charge of money, cash keeper	**cast** (قالب) assign the roles of, choose at random
casual (گاد به گاه) informal, purposeless, occurring by chance	**casualty** (سانحه، کشته) serious or fatal accident, someone injured or killed in an accident
catastrophe (فاجعه) calamity, disaster, state of extreme ruin and misfortune	**category** (دسته بندی) group, class, collection of things sharing a common attribute
cathedral (کلیسای جامع) church, temple	**catholic** (کاتولیک) broadly sympathetic, universal, related to roman catholic church
cause (علت) something produces a result, basis for an action or response, a reason	**caution** (احتیاط) care, being attentive to possible danger
cautious (محتاط) conservative, careful	**cavalry** (سواره نظام) part of military force which serves on horseback
cavern (غار) cave, large underground chamber, as in a cave	**cavity** (حفره) hole, cavern, hollow area within the body
cease (دست کشیدن) stop, terminate, put an end to, discontinue	**celebrate** (جشن گرفتن) praise, assign great social importance to

cell (سلول) any small compartment	**cemetery** (قبرستان) place or ground set apart for the burial of the dead, graveyard
centigrade (درجه سانتیگراد) measure of temperature, used widely in europe	**ceremonial** (تشریفاتی) ritual, ceremony or rite
ceremony (مراسم) formal act or set of acts performed as prescribed by ritual or custom	**certify** (گواهی) give certain information to, assure, make certain
challenge (چالش) assert a right, raise a formal objection, take exception to	**chamber** (محفظه ـ اتاق) cell, compartment, room
champion (قهرمان) protect or fight for as first place	**championship** (قهرمانی) status of being a champion, position or title of a winner
characterize (مشخص کردن) distinguish, be characteristic of, be a distinctive trait or mark of	**chat** (گپ زدن) talk without exchanging too much information, informal conversation
check (بررسی) stop motion, curb or restrain	**cheque** (بررسی) written order directing a bank to pay money
chew (جویدن) bite and grind with the teeth	**chief** (رئیس) highest in office or rank, principal, head
chill (لرز) cool, freeze	**chin** (چانه) central forward portion of the lower jaw, bottom of face
chip (تراشه) cut small pieces from, diminish or reduce to shape, break or crack	**chop** (تکه کردن) hew, cut by striking with a heavy sharp tool, such as an ax

chorus (گروه کر) any utterance produced simultaneously by a group	**circuit** (جریان) electrical device that provides a path for electrical current to flow
circular (گرد) round, shaped like or nearly like a circle	**circulation** (جریان) spread or transmission of something to a wider group or area
circumference (دور) boundary line of a circle, figure, area, or object	**cite** (استناد کنید) quote, adduce as an instance
citizenship (تابعیت) status of a citizen with rights and duties	**civil** (مدنی) having to do with citizens or the state, courteous and polite
claim (مطالبه) demand for something as rightful or due	**clarification** (شفاف سازی) process of making things clearer or easier to understand
clarify (روشن کردن) make clear and comprehensible, elucidate	**clasp** (قلاب) fastening device, firm grip
classification (طبقه بندی) assigning to a class or category	**clay** (گشت) very fine-grained soil that is plastic when moist but hard when fired
clearance (ترخیص کالا از گمرک) act of clearing, space cleared, permission to proceed or trust	**clench** (چنگ زدن) close tightly, grasp or grip tightly, fasten with a clinch
clientele (ارباب رجوع) clients of professional person, body of customers or patrons	**climate** (اقلیم) weather condition, atmosphere, environment
clinic (درمانگاه) healthcare facility for outpatient care	**clip** (کلیپ) small section of filmed or filed material

closet (کمد لباس) small room or apartment, room for privacy	**clumsy** (دست و پا چلفتی) awkward, showing lack of skill or aptitude
clutch (کلاچ) grasp and hold tightly, attempt to grasp or seize	**coach** (مربی ورزشی) tutor, teacher, a vehicle carrying many passengers
coarse (درشت) rough, harsh, of low, common, or inferior quality	**cohesion** (انسجام) tendency to keep together
cohesive (منسجم) cohering or tending to cohere, well integrated	**coin** (سکه) make pieces of money from metal, invent or fabricate
coincide (مصادف شدن) occur at the same time as, correspond	**coincidence** (اتفاقی) two or more things occurring at the same time by chance
coincident (تصادف) concerning, simultaneous	**collaborate** (همکاری) work together, especially in a joint intellectual effort
collapse (سقوط ـ فروپاشی) breakdown, failure	**colleague** (همکار) fellow worker, associate, co-worker
collective (جمعی) common, assembled into or viewed as a whole	**collision** (برخورد) crash, conflict of opposed ideas or attitudes or goals
colonel (سرهنگ) a commissioned military officer	**colonial** (استعماری) of or relating to or characteristic of or inhabiting a colony
combat (مبارزه کن) struggle as with an opposing force, fight with	**combination** (ترکیب) blend, union

combine (ترکیب) blend, fuse, merge	**comedy** (کمدی) light and humorous drama with a happy ending
comic (کمیک) arousing or provoking laughter, ridiculous, amusing, humorous	**commander** (فرمانده) chief, leader
commemorate (بزرگداشت) serve as a memorial to, honor the memory of with a ceremony	**commence** (شروع می شود) have a beginning or origin, originate, start, begin
comment (اظهار نظر) express an opinion, remark	**commerce** (تجارت) trade, business, intellectual exchange or social interaction
commercial (تجاری) money-making, involved in work that is intended for the mass market	**commit** (مرتکب شدن) do something that cannot be changed, cause to be admitted
commitment (تعهد) pledge, undertaking, act of binding yourself to a course of action	**committee** (کمیته) special group delegated to consider some matter
commodity (کالا) goods, article of trade, advantage, benefit.	**commonplace** (عادی) ordinary, having no remarkable features
communicate (برقراری ارتباط) send information about, make known, impart, reveal clearly	**communication** (ارتباطات) activity of communicating, activity of conveying information
companion (همراه و همدم) associate, partner	**company** (شرکت) team, guard team, group of persons, business enterprise
comparable (قابل مقایسه) similar or equivalent, being of equal regard, worthy to be ranked with	**comparative** (مقایسه ای) relative, based on, or involving comparison

comparatively (نسبتاً) relatively, in comparison	**compare** (مقَایسه کنید) examine and note the similarities or differences of
compatible (سازگار) harmonious, having similar disposition and tastes	**compel** (اجبار) force, coerce, necessitate or pressure by force
compensate (جبران کردن) make amends for, reimburse	**compete** (رقابت) contest, fight
competent (صالح) capable, adept	**competition** (رقابت) struggle, rivalry, act of competing as for profit or a prize
complain (شکایت) make a formal accusation, bring a formal charge	**complaint** (شکایت) expression of pain, dissatisfaction, or resentment, criticism
complement (متمم) complete, consummate, make perfect	**compliance** (انطباق) readiness to yield, happy friendly agreement
complicated (بغرنج) difficult to analyze or understand	**component** (جزء) element, ingredient, abstract part of something
composite (کامپوزیت) made up of distinct parts or elements, compounded	**composition** (ترکیب بندی) makeup, constitution, writing, essay
compound (ترکیب) combine, mix, constitute, pay interest, increase	**comprehend** (درک کردن) take in the meaning, nature, or importance of, grasp
comprehension (درک مطلب) grasp, ability to understand	**comprehensive** (همه جانبه) thorough, including all or everything, broad in scope

compress	**comprise**
(فشرده کردن)	(تشکیل می دهند)
close, squeeze or press together, contract	include, consist of, be composed of
compulsory	**compute**
(اجباری)	(محاسبه)
mandatory, obligatory, required by rule	reckon, make mathematical calculation
conceal	**concede**
(پنهان کردن، پوشاندن)	(قبول کردن)
keep from being seen, found, observed, or discovered, secrete	admit, yield, give up physical control of another
conceit	**concept**
(اعتماد به نفس)	(مفهوم)
overly high self-esteem, feelings of excessive pride	something formed in the mind, thought or notion
conception	**concern**
(دریافت، آبستنی)	(نگرانی)
beginning, forming of an idea, act of conceiving	interest in any person or thing, regard, solicitude, anxiety
concerted	**concession**
(پیوند هماهنگ)	(امتیاز)
planned or accomplished together, combined	act of yielding, point yielded, acknowledgment or admission
concise	**conclusive**
(مختصر)	(نتیجه گیری)
brief and compact, expressing much in few words	definitive, decisive, final
concurrent	**condemn**
(هم زمان)	(محکوم کردن)
simultaneous, coincident, occurring or operating at the same time	blame, denounce, express strong disapproval of
condition	**cone**
(وضعیت)	(مخروط)
mode or state of being, fitness, existing circumstances	a shape whose base is a circle and whose sides taper up to a point
conference	**confess**
(کنفرانس)	(اعتراف)
meeting for consultation or discussion, exchange of views	acknowledge, admit

confession (اعتراف) public declaration of faith	**confidence** (اعتماد به نفس) feeling secure or certain about something
confident (مطمئن) assured, having or marked by assurance	**confidential** (محرمانه) treated with confidence, trusted in, trustworthy, secret
confirm (تایید) support or establish the certainty or validity of, verify	**confirmation** (تاییدیه) additional proof that something that was believed
conflict (تعارض) fight, struggle, incompatibility of dates or events	**conformity** (انطباق) similarity in form or character, agreement
confront (روبرو شدن با) be face to face with, oppose in hostility or competition, deal with	**congratulation** (تبریک) act of acknowledging that someone has an occasion for celebration
congress (کنگره) meeting of elected or appointed representatives	**consciousness** (آگاهی) having knowledge of , special awareness or sensitivity:
consecutive (پیاپی) following one after another without interruption, sequential	**consequently** (در نتیجه) therefore, as a result or consequence of something, subsequently
conservation (حفاظت) preservation or restoration from loss, damage, or neglect	**conservative** (محافظه کار) favoring traditional views and values, tending to oppose change
considerable (قابل توجه) worthy of consideration, large in amount, extent, or degree	**considerably** (به طور قابل توجهی) substantially, significantly, to a degree worth considering
considerate (ملاحظه) thoughtful, marked by consideration or reflection, deliberate	**consideration** (توجه) considerate and thoughtful act

consist
(تشکیل شده است از)
be made up or composed, be comprised or contained in

consistency
(ثبات)
harmonious uniformity or agreement among things or parts

consistent
(استوار)
being in agreement with itself, coherent, regular

consonant
(صامت)
compatible, harmonious

conspicuous
(آشکار)
noticeable, prominent, easy to notice, obvious

constant
(مقدار ثابت)
invariable, repeating, continually occurring, persistent

constituent
(تشکیل دهنده)
component or part, citizen, voter

constitute
(تشکیل می دهند)
make up, form something

constraint
(محدودیت)
something that restricts or confines within prescribed bounds

construct
(ساختن)
form by assembling or combining parts, build, create

construction
(ساخت و ساز)
act of constructing or building something

consult
(مشورت کردن)
seek advice or information of, take into account, consider

consultant
(مشاور)
an expert who gives advice

consume
(مصرف کردن)
devour, eat

consumer
(مصرف کننده)
people who buy goods or services

consumption
(مصرف)
eating or drinking of something

contact
(مخاطب)
get in touch with, reach

contain
(حاوی)
include, incorporate, be capable of holding

container
(ظرف)
any object that can be used to hold things

contemporary
(امروزی)
modern, belonging to the same period of time

contemptuous (تحقیر آمیز) scornful, expressing contempt, showing a lack of respect	**content** (محتوا) volume, something contained, material, including text and images
contest (مسابقه) contend for, call in question, oppose, dispute	**continent** (قاره) one of the large landmasses of the earth
continental (قاره) being or concerning or limited to a continent	**contract** (قرارداد) constrict, make smaller, compress or concentrate
contrast (تضاد) act of distinguishing by comparing differences	**contribute** (مشارکت) provide, bestow a quality on
controversial (بحث برانگیز) controvertible, disputable	**convenience** (راحتی) state of being suitable
conventional (مرسوم) based upon tradition rules, formed by agreement or compact	**converse** (مکالمه) chat, talk informally, engage in a spoken exchange of thoughts
conversely (متقابلا) in a converse manner, with change of order or relation, reciprocally.	**convert** (تبدیل) change something into another form, transform
convict (محکوم) find or declare guilty	**convinced** (متقاعد) certain, sure
cooperate (همکاری کردن) work or act together toward a common end or purpose	**cooperation** (مشارکت) practice of cooperating, joint operation or action
cooperative (تعاونی) done with or working with others	**coordinate** (هماهنگ کردن) bring order and organization to, harmonize

cordial (قلبی) gracious, showing warm and friendliness	**core** (هسته) basic, center, or most important part, essence
corn (ذرت) single seed of certain plants, as wheat, grain, small, hard particle	**corner** (گوشه) position at which two lines, surfaces, or edges meet and form an angle
corporation (شرکت) business firm, a group of people combined into or acting as one body	**correlation** (همبستگی) mutual relationship, interdependence or interconnection relationship
correspond (مطابقت) be compatible, similar or consistent, exchange messages	**correspondence** (مکاتبات) similarity or analogy, communication by the exchange of letters
cosmic (کیهانی) pertaining to the universe, vast	**cosmopolitan** (شهری) sophisticated, of worldwide scope
cosmos (کیهان) universe or universality of created things, ordered, harmonious whole	**couch** (نیمکت) sofa, arrange or dispose as in a bed
counsel (مشاوره) advise, suggest	**countenance** (چهره) give sanction or support to, tolerate or approve
counterpart (همتا) duplicate copy, analogue, one that closely resembles another	**countless** (بی شمار) innumerable, infinite, too many to count
coverage (پوشش) extent to which something is covered, news as presented by reporters	**coward** (ترسو) person who lacks courage to face danger, timid
crab (خرچنگ) a stroke of the oar that either misses the water or digs too deeply	**craft** (مهارت) something made by people, vessel

crawl (خزیدن) move slowly, as people or animals with the body near the ground	**crazy** (دیوانه) affected with madness, insane, deranged
create (ایجاد کردن) make or cause to be or to become, invest with a new thing	**creek** (نهر) small stream, often a shallow tributary to a river, brook
creep (خزیدن) move slowly, move stealthily or cautiously	**crook** (کلاه بردار) bend, turn, or curve, curvature, flexure
crooked (کج) having or marked by bends or angles, not straight or aligned, curved	**crumble** (فرو ریختن) break into small pieces, cause to fall in pieces
crust (پوسته) outer layer , covering, coat, shell	**crystal** (کریستال) quartz, glassware made of quartz, high-quality, clear, colorless glass
cubic (مکعب) having three dimensions	**cultivation** (زراعت) production of food by preparing the land to grow crops
cunning (حیله گر) knowing, skillful, artful, designing, deceitful	**cupboard** (کابینت) a small room or cabinet used for storage space
curb (محدود کردن) bend or curve, guide and manage, or restrain	**curiosity** (کنجکاوی) desire to know or learn
currency (واحد پول) money, general acceptance or use	**current** (جاری) stream, flow, up-to-date, present
currently (در حال حاضر) presently, at the present time	**curtail** (کم) cut short or reduce, cut off end or tail, or any part

cushion (کوسن) soft pillow or pad usually used for sitting, reclining, or kneeling	**custom** (سفارشی) tradition, practice followed by people of a particular group or region
customary (مرسوم) agreeing with or established by common usage, conventional, habitual	**customer** (مشتری) patron, one that buys goods or services
customs (گمرک) money collected under a tariff	**dagger** (خنجر) knife, short pointed weapon with sharp edges
dairy (لبنیات) place where milk is produced, kept, or converted into butter or cheese	**damp** (مرطوب) humid, moist, slightly wet
dangerous (خطرناک) full of risk, perilous, hazardous, unsafe	**daring** (شجاعانه) bold, brave
dart (دارت) move suddenly and rapidly	**date** (تاریخ) mark the time of, assign a date to
dawn (سپیده دم) time each morning at which daylight first begins, beginning, start	**dazzling** (خیره کننده) bright, brilliant
deadly (مرگبار) fatal, lethal, causing or tending to cause death	**debate** (مناظره) discussion, dispute, discussion involving opposing points
decade (دهه) a group of ten, especially a period of ten years	**deceive** (فریب) fool, cause to believe what is not true, mislead
decent (نجیب) suitable, modest., honorable, meeting accepted standards	**deception** (فریب) act of deceiving

decimal (اعشاری) of tens, numbered or proceeding by tens, based on ten	**declaration** (اعلام) announcement, explicit statement, formal public statement
decorate (تزئین کنید) adorn, embellish	**decoration** (تزیین) act of decorating something, something used to beautify
decrease (نزول کردن) lessen, reduce, make a quantity smaller	**decree** (حکم) order from one having authority, decision, order, or sentence by court
dedicate (وقف کن) set apart for a deity or for special purposes, devote, consecrate	**deed** (سند ـ سند قانونی) something that is carried out, act or action, feat or exploit
default (پیش فرض) failure to act, an option that is selected automatically	**defeat** (شکست) disfigure, destroy, frustrate, overcome or vanquish, resist with
defect (کاستی) abandon or turn against, cease or change one's loyalty	**defective** (نقَص) having a defect, faulty, imperfect, incomplete, lacking
defence (دفاع) act of defending against attack, danger, or injury	**defend** (دفاع) make or keep safe from danger, attack, or harm
defiance (سرپیچی) refusal to yield, readiness to contend or resist	**deficient** (دارای کمبود) inadequate, lacking an essential quality or element
definite (قطعی) fixed, exact, having distinct limits	**definitely** (قطعاً) unequivocally, clearly, without question and beyond doubt
definition (تعریف) clarity of outline, concise explanation	**definitive** (قطعی) final, complete, precisely defined or explicit

deflate
(فرو رفتگی)
reduce from an inflated condition, release contained air or gas from

deform
(تغییر شکل)
change shape by stress, become misshapen, make formless

deformation
(تغییر شکل)
alteration in the shape or dimensions, a change for the worse

defray
(دزد)
pay costs of, undertake payment of, make compensation to or for

delay
(تاخیر انداختن)
act later than planned, put off, adjournment

delegate
(نماینده)
person authorized to act as representative for another, deputy

delete
(حذف)
erase, strike out, remove or make invisible

delinquency
(بزهکاری)
failure or omission of duty, fault, misdeed, offense or crime

deliver
(ارائه)
set free from restraint, set at liberty, release, give or transfer

delusion
(توهم)
false belief, mistaken or unfounded opinion

demolition
(تخریب)
act of overthrowing, pulling down, or destroying

demonstrate
(نشان دادن)
show clearly and deliberately, manifest, confirm, prove

demonstration
(تظاهرات)
proof, act of showing or making evident

denounce
(محکوم کردن)
condemn openly, criticize, make known in formal manner

dense
(متراکم)
thick, crowded closely together, compact

dent
(دندانه)
cavity, a depression scratched or carved into a surface

dentist
(دندانپزشک)
a person qualified to practice dentistry

deny
(انکار)
disagree with, refuse, declare untrue

depart
(ترک)
take off, leave, set out

departure
(عزیمت، خروج)
act of departing

dependable (قابل اعتماد) reliable, worthy of being depended on, trustworthy	**dependence** (وابستگی) reliance, lack of independence or self-sufficiency
dependent (وابسته) relying on or requiring the aid of another for support	**deplete** (خالی کردن) decrease fullness of, use up or empty out
deposit (سپرده) money given as a guarantee or security	**depreciation** (استهلاک) devaluation, decrease in price or value
depress (افسردگی) lower in spirits, press down	**depressed** (افسرده) sad, gloomy, low in spirits, dejected
deprive (محروم کردن) deny, take away	**derive** (استخراج) obtain or receive from a source, trace the origin or development of
descendant (نسل) offspring, person considered as descended from some ancestor or race	**description** (شرح) act of describing, sketch or account of anything in words
desert (کویر) area with little or no vegetation, forsake, abandon	**deserve** (سزاوار) be worthy of, have a right to
designate (تعیین کردن) indicate or specify, point out, assign a name or title to	**desirable** (مطلوب) worthwhile, worth doing or achieving, advisable
desire (میل) anything which is longing for	**desolate** (متروک) unpopulated, providing no shelter or sustenance, devoid of inhabitants
despair (ناامیدی) loss of hope, utter hopelessness, complete despondency	**desperate** (مستأصل) having lost all hope, dangerous, extremely intense

despise (خوار شمردن) dislike intensely, regard with contempt or scorn	**dessert** (دسر) a dish served as the last course of meal
destination (مقصد) ultimate goal, place to which one is going or directed	**destine** (سرنوشت) decree or designate beforehand, fate
destiny (سرنوشت) event that will inevitably happen in the future	**destruction** (تخریب) havoc, event that completely destroys something
destructive (مخرب) devastating, ruinous	**detect** (تشخیص) feel, discover the presence of, identify
detection (تشخیص) act of detecting, being open what was concealed or hidden, discovery	**deteriorate** (بدتر شدن) become worse, decline
detour (انحراف) a turning, circuitous route, deviation from a direct course	**detriment** (ضرر) harm, damage, injury, something that causes damage, harm, or loss
detrimental (مضر) causing damage or harm, injurious	**deviate** (منحرف شدن) turn away from a principle, norm, depart, diverge
devise (ابداع) form, plan, or arrange in the mind, transmit or give by will	**devotion** (تعلق خاطر) faithfulness, ardent, often selfless affection and dedication
devour (خوردن) consume, eat greedily, destroy completely	**diagnosis** (تشخیص) art of identifying disease, critical analysis of nature of something
diagram (نمودار) graph, chart, figure or drawing made to illustrate a statement, plan	**dialect** (گویش) vocabulary that is for a specific group of people

diction
(نقّاشی)

choice and use of words in speech or writing

diet
(رژیم غذایی)

nutritional plan, nourishment, a prescribed selection of foods

differ
(فرق داشتن)

be or stand apart, disagree, be unlike, be distinguished

digest
(هضم)

break down, make more concise, convert food into absorbable substances

digital
(دیجیتال)

of or performance to fingers, or to digits, done with the fingers

dignity
(کرامت)

quality or state of being worthy of esteem or respect.

diligent
(کوشا)

assiduous, industrious, hard-working

dim
(اذعان)

emitting only a small amount of light, lacking in brightness

dimensional
(ابعادی)

of or relating to dimensions

diminish
(کاهش)

dwindle, reduce, make smaller or less or to cause to appear so

dingy
(گنگ)

darkened with smoke and grime, dirty or discolored

diploma
(دیپلم)

document certifying the successful completion of a course of study

diplomacy
(دیپلماسی)

tact, politics, negotiation between nations

disable
(غیرفعال کردن)

deprive of capability or effectiveness, unable, impair, diminish

disadvantage
(عیب)

drawback, defect, hinder, unfavorable condition or circumstance

disappointment
(ناامیدی)

feeling of dissatisfaction

disapproval
(رد)

a feeling of disliking something or what someone is doing

disaster
(فاجعه)

catastrophe, misfortune

disastrous
(فاجعه بار)

extremely bad, terrible, dreadful

disc
(دیسک)

flat round plate, circular structure either in plants or animals

discard (دور انداختن) throw out something from one's hand, get rid of	**discount** (تخفیف) give reduction in price on
discourage (دلسرد کردن) depress, take away hope from	**discourse** (گفتمان) formal, lengthy discussion of a subject, verbal exchange, conversation
discreet (باهوش) free from ostentation or pretension, distinct, distinguishable	**discrepancy** (اختلاف) lack of consistency, difference
disdain (تحقیر کردن) view with scorn or contempt, feel with aversion	**disgrace** (ننگ) state of dishonor, bring shame or dishonor upon
disguise (مبدل کردن) dress or exterior put on for purposes of concealment or of deception	**disgust** (انزجار) strong feelings of dislike, offend the taste or moral sense of
disinclined (متمایز) not inclined, having a disinclination, being unwilling	**dismal** (ننگین) causing gloom or depression, dreary, somber, melancholy
disorder (بی نظمی) neglect of order or system, irregularity, disturbance, sickness	**dispel** (برطرف کردن) scatter, drive away, cause to vanish
dispense (دفع) distribute, prepare and give out, deal out in parts or portions	**displacement** (جابه جایی) act of removing from office or employment
dispute (اختلاف نظر) argument, angry altercation, quarrel, verbal controversy, debate	**dissipate** (از هم پاشیدن) spend or expend wastefully, vanish by dispersion, drive away, disperse
distant (غیر صمیمی) far in space or time, cold in manner	**distinct** (متمایز) definite, separate, different

distinctly (مجزا) clear to the mind, in a distinct way	**distinguish** (تمیز دادن) characterize, differentiate, recognize
distortion (اعوجاج) mistake of misrepresenting the facts	**distress** (پریشانی) discomfort, cause strain, anxiety, or suffering to
distribute (توزیع کردن) hand out, disseminate, allocate	**distribution** (توزیع) act of distributing or spreading or apportioning
disturbance (مزاحمت) disorder, turmoil, mental or emotional unbalance or disorder	**dive** (شیرجه زدن) plunge, especially headfirst, into water, plummet
diver (غواص) one who works underwater	**diverge** (واگرایی) vary, go in different directions from the same point
diverse (گوناگون، متنوع) differing in some characteristics, various	**diversion** (انحراف) act of turning aside, pastime, activity that relaxes or entertains
diversity (تنوع) point or respect in which things differ, difference	**divert** (منحرف کردن) distract, withdraw money and move into a different location
divine (الهی) perceive intuitively, foresee future, have nature of or being a deity	**divorce** (طلاق) end a marriage, legal dissolution of a marriage
dizzy (سرگیجه) having or causing a whirling sensation	**dock** (حوض) deprive someone of benefits, remove or shorten the tail of an animal
document (سند) provide written evidence, record in detail	**documentation** (مستندات) confirmation that some fact or statement is true

doll
(عروسک)
small toy with human figure, normally for little child

domestic
(داخلی)
house-hold, of or relating to the home , within the country or home

dominant
(غالب)
major, important, outweighing

dominate
(چیره شدن)
monopolize, command, rule, prevail, be prevalent in

donate
(اهدا)
grant, present as a gift to a fund or cause, contribute

donation
(کمک مالی)
grant, act of giving to a fund or cause

dose
(دوز)
quantity of medicine given, sufficient quantity, portion

doubt
(شک)
being in uncertainty as to belief respecting anything

downtown
(مرکز شهر)
commercial center of a town or city

draft
(پیش نویس)
rough outline, draw up an outline, sketch

drag
(کشیدن)
move or bring by force or with great effort

drain
(زه کشی)
draw out, flow out, waste

drainage
(زه کشی)
emptying accomplished by draining, gradual flowing off, as of a liquid

drama
(نمایش)
play, literary work intended for theater

dramatic
(نمایشی)
striking, sensational in appearance or thrilling in effect

drastic
(شدید)
radical, taking effect violently or rapidly

drawing
(نقاشی)
creation of artistic drawings

dread
(وحشت)
fearful or distasteful anticipation, terror, horror

dreadful
(وحشتناک)
very unpleasant, distasteful or shocking

dreary
(رؤیایی)
gloomy, dismal, dark, colorless, or cheerless

drift
(رانش)
float, moving aimlessly, wander

drought
(خشکسالی)
dry period, aridity, long period of abnormally low rainfall

dull
(کدر)
lacking responsiveness or alertness, intellectually weak or obtuse

duly
(بطور درست)
as it ought to be, properly, regularly

dumb
(بی عقل)
mute, lacking the power of speech

dump
(زباله)
sell at artificially low prices, throw away as refuse

durable
(بادوام)
lasting, long-lasting, enduring

dwarf
(آدم کوتوله)
cause to seem small, check natural growth or development of

dwell
(ساکن)
live as a resident, exist in a given place or state

dweller
(ساکن)
a person who inhabits a particular place

dwelling
(سکونت)
residence, place to live in, abode

dye
(رنگ)
substance used to color materials

dynamic
(پویا)
energetic, vigorously active

eager
(مشتاق)
avid, enthusiastic

earnest
(صادقانه)
seriousness, reality, fixed determination, eagerness, intentness

ease
(سهولت)
satisfaction, pleasure, entertainment, freedom from care

eclipse
(گرفتگی)
darken, exceed in importance, outweigh

ecology
(بوم شناسی)
science of the relationships between organisms and their environments

economic
(اقتصادی)
pertaining to economy, frugal, cheap

economize
(اقتصادی کردن)
save money or resource, cut back, be thrifty

ecstasy (وجد) intense joy or delight, any overpowering emotion	**edge** (حاشیه، غیرمتمرکز) brink, perimeter, margin
editorial (سرمقاله) of or pertaining to an editor, written or sanctioned by an editor	**effective** (تاثیرگذار) efficient, productive, producing a strong impression or response
effectiveness (اثربخشی) efficiency, quality of being effective	**eject** (بیرون انداختن) put out or expel from a place, discharge
elbow (آرنج) hinge joint between the forearm and upper arm	**election** (انتخابات) voting, balloting, right or ability to make a choice
electrical (برقی) pertaining to electricity, electric	**electron** (الکترون) elementary particle with negative charge
electronic (الکترونیکی) of or pertaining to an electron or electrons.	**elegance** (ظرافت) refined quality of gracefulness and good taste
elegant (ظریف) refined and tasteful in appearance or behavior or style	**elementary** (ابتدایی) basic, fundamental
elevate (بالا بردن) raise, give a promotion to or assign to a higher position	**elevation** (ارتفاع) altitude, height
elevator (آسانسور) lifting device consisting of a platform or cage	**eliminate** (از بین بردن) eradicate, abolish, rule out
elimination (حذف) act of removing or getting rid of something	**elliptical** (بیضوی) rounded like an egg, in a shape reminding of an ellipse, oval

eloquence (فصاحت) powerful and effective language, persuasive speech	**eloquent** (شیوا) vividly or movingly expressive, persuasive
emancipate (رهایی) free from bondage, oppression, or restraint, liberate	**emancipation** (آزادی) freeing someone from the control of another
embargo (تحریم) ban on commerce or other activity	**embark** (سوار شدن) commence, go on board a boat or airplane, begin a journey
embroider (گلدوزی) decorate with needlework, add details to	**emerge** (ظهور) come into prominence, spring up, appear
emigrant (مهاجر) someone who leaves one country to settle in another	**emission** (انتشار) radiation, discharge, act of emitting
emit (بیرون ریختن) give off, send out, give out as sound	**emotion** (هیجانی) feeling, mood, state of mental agitation or disturbance
emotional (عاطفی) sentimental, passionate, excitable, easily moved	**emphasis** (تاکید) special attention or effort directed toward something, stress
empirical (تجربی) derived from experiment and observation rather than theory	**employ** (اشتغال) engage the services of, put to work, apply
employer (کارفرما) a person or firm that employs workers	**enchant** (مسحور) charm by sorcery, get control of by magical words and rites
encircle (محاصره) form a circle about, enclose within a circle or ring, surround	**enclose** (محصور کردن) include, surround on all sides, close in

enclosure	**encounter**
(محفظہ)	(روبارویی)
place where animals are kept	face, confront, meet, especially unexpectedly, come upon
endeavor	**endless**
(تلاش)	(بی پایان)
attempt by employing effort	without end, having no end or conclusion, perpetual, interminable
endurance	**endure**
(تحمل)	(تحمل کن)
perseverance, state or fact of persevering, continuing existence	tolerate, carry on through, despite hardships
energetic	**engulf**
(پرانرژی)	(درگیر)
active, brisk, vigorous	absorb or swallow up as in a gulf, flow over or cover completely
enhance	**enormous**
(تَقویت)	(عظیم)
make better or more attractive, increase, improve	very great in size, extent, number, or degrees, huge, massive
enquiry	**enterprise**
(استعلام)	(شرکت، پروژہ)
search for knowledge, systematic investigation	company, firm, organization created for business ventures
entertain	**enthusiastic**
(سرگرمی)	(مشتاق)
amuse, host	having or showing great excitement and interest
entrance	**entreat**
(ورود)	(دعا)
fill with delight or wonder, put into a trance, attract	plead, make earnest request of, ask for earnestly
entry	**enumerate**
(ورود)	(شمردن)
admission, entrance, item inserted in a written record	list each one, mention one by one
envelop	**epoch**
(پاکت نامہ)	(دورہ)
enclose or encase completely with or as if with a covering	particular period of history, especially one considered remarkable

equal
(برابر)
having the same quantity, measure, or value as another, identical

equality
(برابری)
state or quality of being equal

equation
(معادله)
making equal, equal division, equality, equilibrium

equivalent
(معادل)
interchangeable, comparable, equal, as in value, force, or meaning

eradicate
(ریشه کن کردن)
completely destroy, eliminate, exterminate

erase
(پاک کردن)
rub letters or characters written, engraved, or painted

erect
(ساخت)
construct, stand, set up

erosion
(فرسایش)
corrosion, a gradual decline of something

errand
(کارهای محوله)
short trip taken to perform a specified task, mission, embassy

eruption
(فوران)
outbreak, sudden, often violent outburst

escalator
(پله برقی)
stairway whose steps move continuously on a circulating belt

essence
(ذات)
most essential or most vital part of some idea or experience

establish
(تأسیس کردن)
set up or found, build

estate
(املاک)
extensive landed property, everything you own, all of your assets

esteem
(احترام)
regard with respect, favorable regard

estimate
(تخمین زدن)
judge to be probable, form an opinion about, evaluate

evaluate
(ارزیابی)
judge, examine and judge carefully, appraise

evaporate
(تبخیر کنید)
vaporize, disappear, change into a vapor

evaporation
(تبخیر)
process of extracting moisture

eventful
(واقعه انگیز)
busy, momentous, full of events or incidents

eventually (در نهایت) ultimately, in the final result or issue, in the end	**everlasting** (جاودانه) continuing forever or indefinitely
evidence (شواهد و مدارک) something which makes evident or manifest, any mode of proof	**evolution** (سیر تکاملی) development, progression
exact (دقیق) precisely agreeing with standard, fact, or truth, perfectly conforming	**exaggeration** (اغراق) overstatement, act of making something more noticeable than usual
exasperate (عجیب) make worse, irritate, make very angry or impatient, annoy greatly	**exceed** (تجاوز) go beyond, be or do something to a greater degree
exceedingly (بسیار زیاد) in a very great degree, beyond what is usual, surpassingly	**excel** (برتری داشتن) be superior, distinguish oneself
exception (استثنا) instance that does not conform to a rule	**exceptional** (استثنایی) extraordinary, unusual, well above average
excess (اضافی) amount or quantity beyond what is normal or sufficient, surplus	**excessive** (بیش از اندازه) extreme, inordinate, too much
exchange (تبادل) substitute, trade in, give in return for something received	**excitement** (هیجان) state of being emotionally aroused
exciting (هیجان انگیز) creating or producing excitement	**exclaim** (بانگ زدن) cry out suddenly, as from surprise or emotion
exclude (رد کردن) leave out of, keep out of, reject	**exclusion** (محرومیت) rejection, act of excluding or shutting out

exclusively (منحصراً) without any others being included or involved, purely, strictly	**excursion** (گشت و گذار) trip, usually short journey made for pleasure
execute (اجرا کردن) put into effect, carry out the legalities of	**execution** (اعدام) accomplishment, putting into practice, putting a person to death
exempt (معافیت) not subject to duty or obligation, not subject to taxation	**exert** (اعمال) cause, apply, exercise
exertion (فشار) effort, expenditure of much physical work	**exhausted** (خسته) depleted, tired
exhaustive (جامع) treating all parts or aspects without omission, comprehensive	**exhibition** (نمایشگاه) exposition, presentation, large-scale public showing
exile (تبعید) force separation from one's native country	**exit** (خروج) passage or way out, act of going away or out
exonerate (تبرئه کردن) acquit, free from blame, discharge from duty	**expand** (بسط دادن) become larger in size or volume, grow stronger, add details
expansion (انبساط) growth, extent or amount by which something has expanded	**expedient** (مصلحت) suitable, appropriate to a purpose, serving to promote your interest
expedition (اعزامی) journey organized for a particular purpose	**expel** (اخراج) oust, discharge, force or drive out
expenditure (هزینه) payment or expense, output	**expertise** (تجربه و تخصص) specialized knowledge, expert skill

explode (منفجر شدن) erupt, blow up, burst violently as a result of internal pressure	**exploitation** (بهره برداری) unfair use of someone's work giving little in return
exploration (اکتشاف) travel for the purpose of discovery	**explorer** (کاوشگر) someone who travels into little known regions
explosive (انفجاری) tending or serving to sudden outburst, sudden and loud	**export** (صادرات) sell or transfer abroad
expose (در معرض گذاشتن) set forth, set out to public view	**expressive** (رسا) demonstrative, indicative
exquisite (نفیس) excellent, flawless, acutely perceptive or discriminating	**extend** (توسعه دادن، گسترش) open or straighten something out, unbend, prolong
extension (افزونه) supplement, act of extending or the condition of being extended	**extensive** (گسترده) widespread, far-reaching, wide
exterior (خارجی) outside, external or outward appearance	**external** (بیرونی) exterior, outer, suitable for application to the outside
extinct (منقرض شده) no longer existing or living, vanished, dead	**extinction** (انقراض) death of all its remaining members
extra (اضافی) something additional of the same kind	**extraordinary** (خارق العاده) exceptional, remarkable, beyond what is ordinary or usual
extreme (مفرط) outermost, utmost, farthest, most remote, at the widest limit	**fabricate** (ساختگی) build, put together out of components or parts

face
(صورت)
confront, encounter, be opposite

facilitate
(تسهیل کردن)
help bring about, make less difficult

facility
(امکانات)
service, space, and equipment provided for a particular purpose

faction
(فرقه)
a party of persons having a common end in view

factor
(عامل)
anything that contributes causally to a result, element, variable

fade
(محو شدن)
disappear, die out, lose color, lose freshness

faint
(از هوش رفتن)
lacking strength or vigor , weak

fairy
(پری)
enchantment, illusion, imaginary supernatural being or spirit

faith
(ایمان)
loyalty or allegiance to a cause or a person, complete confidence

fake
(جعلی)
imitation, counterfeit, having a false or misleading appearance

fame
(شهرت)
favorable public reputation, great renown

familiar
(آشنا)
well known or easily recognized

famine
(قحطی)
shortage of food, starvation

fancy
(تفننی)
capricious notion, something many people believe that is false

fantastic
(خارق العاده)
excellent, extraordinary, strange in form, conception, or appearance

fare
(کرایه)
food and drink, diet, transportation charge, a paying passenger

farewell
(بدرود)
acknowledgment at parting, goodbye, act of departing or taking leave

fascination
(شیفتگی)
capacity to attract intense interest

fashion
(روش)
style, shape, appearance, or mode of structure, pattern, model

fasten
(بستن)
attach, affix

fatal (کُشنده) causing death	**fathom** (فتحوم) measure the depth, come to understand
fatigue (خستگی) physical or mental weariness, exhaustion	**fault** (عیب) crack, a crack in the earth, defect, flaw, a wrong action
favorable (مطلوب) approving or pleasing, granting what has been desired or requested	**feasible** (امکان پذیر است) capable of being accomplished or brought about
feat (شاهکار) achievement, accomplishment	**feature** (ویژگی) prominent aspect of something
federal (فدرال) of or relating to central government, national	**federation** (فدراسیون) uniting in a league, confederation, league
fee (هزینه) give a tip beyond the agreed-on compensation	**feeble** (ضعیف) lacking vigor, force, or effectiveness, faint, frail
feed (خوراک) give food to, supply with nourishment	**feedback** (بازخورد) response to an inquiry or experiment
fell (سقوط) capable of destroying, lethal	**female** (زن) for or composed of women or girls
ferocious (وحشی) fierce, savage, wild, indicating cruelty	**ferry** (کشتی) shuttle, transport by boat or aircraft
fertile (حاصلخیز) rich, fruitful, inventive, creative, intellectually productive	**fertilizer** (کود) any substance used to make soil more fertile

fervent (خونسرد) extremely hot, sincerely or intensely felt	**festival** (جشنواره) a day or period of time for feasting and celebration
fetch (رفتن و آوردن) take away or remove, reduce, go or come after and bring or take back	**feud** (دشمنی) bitter quarrel between two parties
fictional (داستانی) imaginary, invented, as opposed to real	**fierce** (شدید) ferocious, savage, extremely severe or violent, terrible
fig (شکل) small fruit tree with large leaves, known from the remotest antiquity	**figurative** (فیگوراتیو) not literal, but metaphorical, using figure of speech
file (فایل) line, proceed in line	**filthy** (کثیف) nasty, dirty, polluted, foul, impure
final (نهایی) forming or occurring at the end, terminating, ultimate, conclusive	**financial** (مالی) monetary, pertaining or relating to money matters
financing (تأمین مالی) subsidy, transaction that provides funds for a business	**finite** (محدود، فانی) having a limit, limited in quantity, degree, or capacity, bounded
fir (صنوبر) any of various evergreen trees of the genus abies	**firm** (محکم) hard, solid, resolute, determined
fist (مشت) hand with the fingers doubled into the palm, closed hand	**fit** (مناسب) be the right size or shape, conform to some shape or size
fixed (درست شد) firmly in position, stationary	**fixture** (فیکسچر) commonplace object, object firmly fixed in place

flag
(پرچم)
become less intense, sink, or settle from pressure

flare
(شعله ور شدن)
sudden outburst of emotion, glare, shine, shine with sudden light

flavor
(طعم)
distinctive taste, quality produced by the sensation of taste

flee
(فرار)
run away, as from danger or evil, avoid in alarmed or cowardly manner

flexibility
(انعطاف پذیری)
quality of being adaptable or variable

flexible
(قابل انعطاف)
pliant, elastic, capable of being bent or flexed, pliable

float
(شناور)
drift along, make the surface of level or smooth, move lightly

flock
(گله)
group, herd, crowd, gather, crowd, throng

flour
(آرد)
fine powdery foodstuff, soft, fine powder

flourish
(شکوفا شدن)
grow well, decorate with ornaments, be in a period of productivity

fluctuate
(نوسان)
rise and fall in or as if in waves, shift, vary irregularly

fluctuation
(نوسان)
a wave motion

fluency
(تسلط)
quality of smoothness of flow, quality of being fluent in language

flux
(شار)
flowing, series of changes, state of being liquid through heat

fodder
(علوفه)
coarse food for cattle or horses

foe
(دشمن)
enemy, one who entertains hatred, grudge, adversary

fog
(مه)
droplets of water vapor suspended in air near ground , haze

foggy
(مه آلود)
obscured by fog, indistinct or hazy in outline

fold
(تا کردن)
make something double, bend or lay so that one part covers the other

foliage
(شاخ و برگ)
masses of leaves, a cluster of leaves, flowers, and branches

forbid (منع) not allow, prohibit, prevent	**forecast** (پیش بینی) prediction about how something will develop, as for weather
forefather (پدر بزرگ) ancestor, forebear	**foremost** (در درجه نخست) leading, main, primary, first in time or place
foretell (پیشگویی) tell of or indicate beforehand, predict	**forge** (ساختن) workplace where metal is worked by heating and hammering
formal (رسمی) official, executed, carried out, or done in proper or regular form	**format** (قالب) pattern, design, set into a specific pattern
formation (تشکیل) configuration, pattern	**former** (سابق) preceding in order of time, antecedent, previous, prior, earlier
formerly (سابق) previously, at an earlier time, once	**formidable** (نیرومند) arousing fear, threatening, difficult to undertake or defeat
formulate (فرمول) decide upon and express in words	**forsake** (رها کردن) leave someone who needs or counts on you
fort (دژ) a fortified defensive structure, permanent army post	**forthcoming** (آینده) ready or about to appear, making appearance
fortitude (استحکام) bravery, force, power to attack or to resist attack	**fortnight** (دو هفته) a period of fourteen consecutive days
fortunate (خوش شانس) lucky, bringing something good and unforeseen	**forward** (رو به جلو) at or to or toward the front, toward the future

foster
(پرورش دادن، پروردن)

rear, promote the growth of, help develop

foul
(ناپاک)

act that violates of the rules of a sport

founder
(مؤسس)

person who establishes an organization, business

fraction
(کسر)

segment, fragment, a small proportion of

fracture
(شکست، شکستگی)

break into pieces, crack, destroy, violate or abuse

fragile
(شکننده)

easy to destroy, delicate, not strong

fragment
(قطعه)

small part broken off or detached, fraction

fragrance
(عطر)

scent, aroma, distinctive odor that is pleasant

fragrant
(معطر)

pleasant-smelling, odorous

frail
(نحیف)

physically weak, easily broken

framework
(چارچوب)

fundamental structure, as for a written work, skeleton

frank
(صریح)

honest, sincere, open and sincere in expression, straightforward

fret
(اخم کردن)

cause to be uneasy, wear away

friction
(اصطکاک)

clash in opinion, rubbing against, conflict

frightening
(ترسناک)

inspiring with fear, causing fear, of capable of causing fear, scary

frugal
(ناخوشایند)

sparing, economical, costing little, inexpensive

fruitful
(مثمر ثمر)

productive, fertile, producing results, profitable

fuel
(سوخت)

substance that can be consumed to produce energy

function
(عملکرد)

act of executing or performing any duty, assigned duty or activity

functional
(عملکردی)

useful, in good working order

fundamental (اساسی) relating to foundation or base, elementary, primary, essential	**furious** (خشمگین) extreme anger, raging, full of activity, energetic or rapid
further (به علاوه) get greater distance, make more in advance	**furthermore** (علاوه بر این) in addition, moreover, still further
fury (خشم) violent anger, rage, uncontrolled action, turbulence	**fuse** (فیوز) combine, blend, become plastic or fluid or liquefied from heat
gallery (آلبوم عکس) long usually narrow room , covered corridor	**gamble** (قمار) play or game for money or other stake, lose or squander by gaming
gap (شکاف) opening through mountains, pass, conspicuous difference or imbalance	**garbage** (زباله) trash, worthless or nonsensical matter, food wastes
garment (پوشاک) any article of clothing, as coat or gown	**gauge** (پیمانه) measuring instrument, measure, judge
generalize (تعمیم دادن) reach conclusion, become systemic and spread throughout the body	**generate** (تولید می کنند) bring into being, give rise to, produce
generous (سخاوتمندانه) more than adequate, willing to give and share unstintingly	**genuine** (اصل) authentic, real, true
germ (ریشه) bacteria, earliest form of an organism, seed	**giant** (غول) person of extraordinary strength or powers, bodily or intellectual
gigantic (غول پیکر) exceedingly large, huge, very large or extensive	**ginger** (زنجبیل) plant of the genus zingiber, of the east and west indies

glare (تابش خیره کننده) light, brightness, fierce or angry stare	**glassware** (ظروف شیشه ای) an article of tableware made of glass
gleam (سوسو زدن) cause to emit a flash of light	**glide** (سر خوردن) slide, move in a smooth, effortless manner
glimpse (نظر اجمالی) glance, a quick look , see briefly, a brief or incomplete view	**glitter** (زرق و برق) bright, sparkling light, brilliant and showy luster, brilliancy
global (جهانی) worldwide, international, having the shape of a globe	**gloomy** (تاریک) imperfectly illuminated, dusky, dim, clouded
glut (گلوت) fill beyond capacity, especially with food, swallow greedlly	**gnaw** (مانند موش جویدن) bite or chew on with the teeth
goal (هدف) end, objective, final purpose or aim	**gorge** (تپه) stuff oneself, overeat, make a pig of oneself
gorgeous (جذاب) dazzlingly beautiful, magnificent	**governor** (فرماندار) head of a state government
grab (گرفتن) take or grasp suddenly, snatch, capture	**graceful** (برازنده) elegant, showing grace of movement, form, or proportion
gracious (بخشنده) beneficent, merciful, disposed to show kindness or favor	**grand** (عالی) large and impressive in size, scope, or extent
grant (اعطا کردن) allow to have, give on the basis of merit, be willing to concede	**graph** (نمودار) chart, a drawing illustrating the relations

grasp
(فهم)
grip, take hold of or seize firmly with or as if with the hand

grateful
(ممنون)
thankful, appreciative of benefits received

gratify
(خوشحال کردن)
give pleasure to, satisfy, indulge, make happy

gratis
(رایگان)
free, without charge, costing nothing

grave
(قبر)
place for the burial, death or extinction

graze
(چراندن)
scrape gently, feed on growing grasses and herbage

grease
(گریس)
oil, fat, state of being covered with unclean things

greedy
(حریص)
wanting to get more than one can reasonably get

grieve
(اندوه)
cause to be sorrowful, distress

grim
(گریم)
unrelenting, rigid, dismal and gloomy, cold and forbidding

grin
(پوزخند)
act of withdrawing lips and showing teeth, broad smile

grip
(گرفتن)
hold fast or firmly, seize as in a wrestling match

groan
(ناله)
give forth a low, moaning sound in breathing

grope
(افتخار)
search blindly or uncertainly, reach about uncertainly, feel one's way

gross
(ناخالص)
of huge size, excessively large, coarse, rough, not fine or delicate

ground
(زمین)
solid surface of the earth, bottom, lowest part

grove
(بیشه)
group of trees smaller than a forest, orchard

grumble
(غصه خوردن)
utter or emit low dull rumbling sounds

guarantee
(ضمانت)
pledge that something will happen or that something is true

guilty
(گناهکار)
deserving of blame, adjudged to have committed crime

gulf (خليج) an arm of a sea or ocean partly enclosed by land, larger than a bay	**gulp** (خندق) swallow, utter or make a noise, as when swallowing too quickly
gust (هوس) blast, outburst	**haggard** (حياط) wasted away, showing wearing effects of overwork or suffering
haggle (چانه زدن) argue about prices, bargain, as over the price of something	**hail** (تگرگ) call for, salute, greet, praise vociferously
halt (مكث) stop, stand in doubt, hesitate	**ham** (ژامبون) meat cut from the thigh of a hog, usually smoked
hamburger (همبرگر) a fried bread of minced beef served on a bun	**hamper** (مانع) put at disadvantage, prevent progress or free movement of
handbook (كتابچه راهنما) concise reference book providing specific information	**handful** (تعداد انگشت شماری) a small number
handicap (معلوليت) disadvantage, physical disability, cripple, hinder, impede	**handy** (مفيد) convenient, close
harbor (بندرگاه) provide a refuge for, hide, give shelter to	**harden** (سخت شدن) become hard or harder
harmful (زيان آور) damaging, noxious, detrimental, dangerous	**harmonious** (هماهنگ) concordant, accordant, suitable and fitting
harmony (هماهنگى) compatibility in opinion and action, an agreeable sound property	**harsh** (خشن) rough, coarse, severe, unpleasantly stern

harvest (محصول) gather, yield from plants in a single growing season	**haste** (عجله) hurry, rapidity of action or motion
hasty (شتابزده) easily angered, irritable, made too quickly to be accurate or wise	**hatch** (دریچه) breed, emerge from the egg
haul (حمل و نقل) draw slowly or heavily, pull or drag forcibly, shift direction	**haunt** (تعقیب کردن) be a regular or frequent visitor to a certain place, bother, disturb
hawk (شاهین) bird of prey typically having short rounded wings and a long tail	**hay** (یونجه) grass or other plants, cut and dried for fodder
headlong (بی سر) uncontrollably forceful or fast, done with head leading, headfirst	**heal** (شفا دادن) cure, make or get healthy again
heap (پشته) crowd or throng, a great number of persons, pile or mass	**hedge** (پرچین) thicket of bushes, usually thorn bushes
heed (توجه) pay attention to, listen to and consider	**heel** (پاشنه) back part of the human foot, lower end of a ship's mast
heighten (قد بلند) enhance, hoist, raise or increase the quantity or degree of, intensify	**heir** (واری) person who inherits some title or office
heiress (وارث) woman who is an heir, especially to great wealth	**helpless** (درمانده) unable to help oneself, powerless or incompetent, powerless, weak
hemisphere (نیمکره) halves, half of a sphere bounded by a great circle	**herald** (قاصد) proclaim, announces important news, messenger

herb (گیاه دارویی) plant lacking a permanent woody stem, some having medicinal properties	**herd** (گله) flock, crowd, group of cattle or other domestic animals
hesitate (تردید) pause or hold back in uncertainty or unwillingness	**hide** (پنهان شدن) prevent from being seen or discovered
hijack (ربودن) stop and rob a vehicle in transit, seize control of by use of force	**hint** (اشاره) allusion, clue, brief or indirect suggestion
historian (تاریخ شناس) one who is an authority on history	**hoist** (بلند کردن) raise, lift, elevate, raise to one's mouth in order to drink
hold (نگه دارید) keep from departing, take and maintain control over, stop dealing with	**hop** (هاپ) move by successive leaps, as toads do, spring or jump on one foot
horizontal (افقی) flat, level, parallel to or in a base line	**horn** (شیپور) one of the bony outgrowths on the heads of certain ungulates
horrible (ناگوار) exciting, or tending to horror or fear, hideous	**horror** (وحشت) terror, fear, intense dislike
hospitable (مهمان نواز) disposed to treat guests with warmth and generosity, receptive	**host** (میزبان) great number, person entertaining guests
hostile (خصومت آمیز) unfriendly, showing the disposition of an enemy	**house** (خانه) provide living quarters for, lodge, contain, harbor
hover (شناور) hang about, wait nearby, remain floating	**hug** (در آغوش گرفتن) crowd together, keep close to, tight or amorous embrace

hum (هوم) low, prolonged sound, humming noise, singing with shut mouth	**humane** (انسانی) marked by kindness, mercy, or compassion
humanity (بشریت) kindness, virtue, all of the inhabitants of the earth	**humble** (فروتن) low or inferior in station or quality, modest
humid (مرطوب) containing a high amount of water or water vapor	**humidity** (رطوبت) dampness, moisture
humiliate (تحقیر کردن) cause to feel shame, hurt the pride of	**humorous** (طنز) employing or showing humor, funny, amusing
hunger (گرسنگی) strong desire for something, feel the need to eat	**hurl** (شتاب) throw with great force, cast, toss
husband (شوهر) use economically, conserve, save	**hush** (هوس) make silent or quiet, keep from public knowledge, suppress mention of
hustle (فشار) bustle, cause to move furtively and hurriedly	**hypothesis** (فرضیه) assumption, theory
hypothetical (فرضی) based on assumptions, supposed	**identical** (همسان) duplicate, alike, being the exact same one
identify (شناسایی) detect, find out, discover	**idiomatic** (اصطلاحی) having the nature of an idiom, characteristic of a given language
idiot (ادم سفیه و احمق) foolish or stupid person, unlearned, ignorant, or simple person	**ignorance** (جهل) lack of knowledge or education

ignorant (نادان) lacking education or knowledge, unaware	**illegible** (ناخوانا) incapable of being read, unclear, not legible
illusion (توهم) misleading vision, being deceived by a false perception or belief	**illusive** (توهمی) deceptive, misleading, based on or having the nature of an illusion
illustration (تصویر) picture, drawing, showing by example	**image** (تصویر) visual representation, representation of a person
imaginary (خیالی) having existence only in the imagination, fanciful, visionary	**imitation** (تقلید) emulation, copying the actions of someone else
immense (عظیم) enormous, boundless, so great as to be beyond measurement	**immerse** (غوطه وری) plunge into anything, especially a fluid, sink, dip
impact (تأثیر) forceful consequence, strong effect, influencing strongly	**impartial** (بی طرف) not biased, fair, showing lack of favoritism
implement (پیاده سازی) put into effect, supply with tools	**implore** (کاوش کردن) beg for urgently, make an earnest appeal
import (وارد کردن) bring in from another country	**impose** (تحمیل کردن) demand, force, compel to behave in a certain way
impractical (غیر عملی) unwise to implement or maintain in practice, theoretical	**impressive** (چشمگیر) making a strong or vivid impression, producing a strong effect
impulse (ضربه) act of applying force suddenly, an impelling force or strength	**inability** (عجز) lack of ability, especially mental ability, to do something

inadequate

(ناکافی)

not sufficient to meet a need, insufficient, poor

inaugurate

(تحلیف)

start, initiate, induct into office by formal ceremony

incense

(بخور دادن)

enrage, infuriate, cause to be extremely angry

incentive

(تشویق)

something, such as the fear of punishment or the expectation of reward

incidentally

(اتفاقاً)

by chance, accidentally

inclination

(تمایل)

preference, tendency, inclined surface, slope

inclined

(شیب دار)

tending or leaning toward, bent, having preference or tendency

income

(درآمد)

gain from labor, business, property, or capital

inconvenient

(نامناسب)

not suited to your comfort, purpose or needs

incredulous

(بی اعتقاد)

difficult to believe, incredible, skeptical

increment

(افزایش)

process of increasing in number, size, quantity, or extent

incur

(متحمل شدن)

bring upon oneself, become liable to, acquire or come into

indefinite

(نامعین)

unclear, vague, lacking precise limits

indent

(تورفتگی)

nick, set in from margin, impress or stamp

indicate

(نشان دادن)

point out, direct to a knowledge of

indicative

(نشان دهنده)

suggestive, implying, serving to indicate

indifference

(بی تفاوتی)

unconcern, disinterest, lack of enthusiasm

indifferent

(بی تفاوت)

having no particular interest or concern, being neither good nor bad

indispensable

(ضروری)

essential, requisite, impossible to be omitted or remitted

individual

(شخصی)

single person or thing, human regarded as a unique personality

induce (وادار کردن) persuade, bring about, reason or establish by induction	**industrialization** (صنعتی سازی) development of industry on an extensive scale
industrialized (صنعتی) made industrial, converted to industrialism	**industrious** (سخت کوش) diligent, hard-working, busy and laborious
infant (شیرخوار) child in the first period of life, young babe	**infantry** (پیاده نظام) body of children, a body of soldiers serving on foot, foot soldiers
infect (آلوده کردن) bring into contact with a substance that can cause illness	**infectious** (عفونی) contagious, contaminating
inferiority (فرومایگی) state of being lower than or not as good as	**inflation** (تورم) general increase in the prices of goods and services in a country
influential (موثر) important, powerful, having or exercising influence or power	**influenza** (آنفلوانزا) an acute febrile highly contagious viral disease
informal (دوستانه و غیر رسمی) absence of ceremony, casual	**informative** (آموزنده) instructive, illustrative, providing or conveying information
infringe (نقض کردن) act contrary to, as a law, right, or obligation, annul or hinder	**ingenious** (مبتکرانه) clever, having inventive or cunning mind
inhabit (ساکن بودن) live in, occupy, reside in	**inhabitant** (مقیم) resident, someone or thing who lives in a place
inherent (ذاتی) firmly established by nature or habit	**initial** (اولیه) early, preliminary, occurring at the beginning

initially	**initiate**
(در ابتدا)	(آغاز کردن)
in the beginning, at first	begin, originate, admit into membership
inject	**injure**
(تزریق)	(زخمی شدن)
put in, infuse , force or drive fluid into something	do harm to, inflict damage, do injustice to
injury	**innocent**
(صدمه)	(بی گناه)
any physical damage to body caused by violence or accident or fracture	naive, lacking sense or awareness, free from evil or guilt
innovation	**inquiry**
(نوآوری)	(استعلام)
introduction of something new	investigation, search for knowledge
insane	**insert**
(مجنون)	(درج کنید)
exhibiting disordered of mind, deranged in mind, very foolish	input, enter, put or set into, between, or among
insolvent	**inspect**
(ورشکسته)	(بازرسی)
bankrupt, unable to repay one's debts	look over, examine carefully and critically, especially for flaws
inspection	**inspector**
(بازرسی)	(بازرس)
formal or official examination	high ranking police officer, investigator who observes carefully
install	**installment**
(نصب)	(قسط)
set up, connect or set in position and prepare for use	monthly payment, a part of a published serial
instinct	**instinctive**
(غریزه)	(غریزی)
inborn pattern of behavior , nature	unthinking, prompted by instinct, spontaneous
institution	**instruct**
(موسسه، نهاد)	(آموزش)
institute, organization, introducing something new	teach, make aware of

instruction (دستورالعمل) direction, teaching, activities of educating or instructing	**instructive** (آموزنده) serving to instruct of enlighten or inform, enlightening
insufficient (ناکافی) of a quantity not able to fulfill a need or requirement	**insult** (توهین) offend, affront, treat, mention, or speak to rudely
insurance (بیمه) protection against future loss, act, business, or system of insuring	**intangible** (نامشهود) not able to be perceived by senses, as touch, vague
integral (انتگرال) essential or necessary for completeness, entire	**integrate** (ادغام) make whole, combine, make into one unit
integrity (تمامیت) quality or condition of being whole or undivided, completeness	**intellect** (عقل) ability to learn and reason, ability to think abstractly or profoundly
intense (شدید، قوی) extreme, acute, in an extreme degree	**intensive** (متمرکز) thorough, concentrated, tending to give force or emphasis
intent (قصد) something that is intended, aim or purpose	**intention** (قصد) motive, with respect to marriage, aim that guides action
interact (تعامل داشتن) interplay, act together or towards others or with	**interaction** (اثر متقابل) communication, a mutual or reciprocal action, interacting
interest (علاقه) attention, curiosity, dividend, yield	**interfere** (مداخله کردن) disrupt, hinder, be or create a hindrance or obstacle
interior (داخلی) inside, inner part, internal, inner	**intermediate** (حد واسط) middle, lying between two extremes

internal
(درونی؛ داخلی)

inside, interior, located within the limits or surface

interpret
(تفسیر)

explain or tell the meaning of, translate orally, decipher

interrupt
(قطع کردن)

terminate, make a break in

interval
(فاصله)

pause, break, space between two objects, points, or units

intervene
(دخالت)

get involved, come, appear, or lie between two things

intrude
(مزاحمت)

trespass, enter as an uninvited person

inundate
(فرو ریختن)

overwhelm, cover with water, especially floodwaters

invade
(حمله)

move into, intrude, enter by force in order to conquer or pillage

invader
(مهاجم)

one who invades, assailant, encroacher, intruder

invalid
(بی اعتبار)

of no force or weight, not valid, weak, void, null

invariably
(به طور همیشگی)

constantly, always

inverse
(معکوس)

opposite, reversed in order, nature, or effect, turned upside down

investigate
(تحقیق کردن)

explore, observe or inquire into in detail, examine systematically

investigation
(تحقیق و بررسی)

detailed inquiry or systematic examination, inquiry

invisible
(نامرئی)

incapable of being seen, impossible or nearly impossible to see

irregular
(بی رویه)

contrary to rule or accepted order or general practice, inconstant

irresistible
(مقاومت ناپذیر)

overwhelming, tempting, charming

irrigate
(آبیاری)

supply land with water artificially, clean a wound with a fluid

irrigation
(آبیاری)

supplying water to the land to help crops grow

irritate
(تحریک کردن)

rouse to impatience or anger, annoy, provoke

isolate (منزوی) seclude, set apart or cut off from others	**isolation** (انزوا) separation, detachment, quality or condition of being isolated
issue (موضوع) subject, topic, problem, edition, publication, release, publish	**ivory** (عاج) teeth of elephant, pale or grayish yellow to yellowish white
jail (زندان) building for confinement of persons held in lawful custody	**jam** (مربا) crush or bruise, get stuck, press tightly together
jealousy (حسادت) envy, jealous attitude or disposition	**jelly** (ژله) substance having the consistency of semi-solid foods
jewel (جواهرات) gemstone, costly ornament of precious metal or gem	**jewelry** (جواهر سازی) adornment made of precious metals, as a bracelet or ring or necklace
jog (آهسته) run or ride at a steady slow trot, give a push or shake to	**journalist** (روزنامه نگار) writer for newspapers and magazines
juice (آب میوه) liquid, liquid part that can be extracted from plant or animal tissue	**juicy** (آبدار) full of juice, lucrative, richly interesting
junction (اتصال) connection, joint, intersection, crossing	**jungle** (جنگل) land densely overgrown with tropical vegetation, dense, confused mass
jury (هیئت داوران) committee appointed to judge a case	**justifiable** (قابل توجیه) capable of being justified, or shown to be just
justification (توجیه) good or just reason, condition or fact of being justified	**kangaroo** (کانگورو) animal that having large powerful hind legs and a long thick tail

keen

(تیز)

acute, incisive, sharp , express grief verbally

kerosene

(نفت سفید)

flammable hydrocarbon oil used as fuel in lamps and heaters

kindle

(روشن شدن)

build or fuel a fire, cause to glow, light up, inspire

kneel

(زانو زدن)

bend the knee, fall or rest on the knees

knob

(دستگیره)

hard protuberance, hard swelling or rising, bunch, lump

laborer

(کارگر)

worker, someone who works with their hands

lag

(تاخیر)

delay, drag, the act of slowing down or falling behind

lamb

(گوشت بره)

the young of the sheep, simple, unsophisticated person

landing

(فرود آمدن)

touchdown, act of coming down to the earth

landscape

(چشم انداز)

scenery, expanse of scenery that can be seen in a single view

lap

(دامان)

take in food or drink with one's tongue, splash gently

largely

(تا حد زیادی)

in a large manner, for the most part, mainly

lasting

(بادوام)

continuing or remaining for a long time, enduring, durable

latent

(نهفته)

present or potential but not evident or active, dormant, hidden

lateral

(جانبی)

coming from side, situated at or extending to the side

launch

(راه اندازی)

begin, originate, initiate, send off, take off

lawn

(چمن)

landscape, grassland, usually tended or mowed, meadow

lay

(درازکشیدن)

put into a certain place, cause to lie down, spread over a surface

layout

(چیدمان)

overall design of a page, plan or design of something that is laid out

leadership

(رهبری)

guidance, direction, authority, position or office of a leader

leading (منتهی شدن) chief, principal, having a position in the lead, foremost	**leaflet** (جزوه) small leaf, leaf like organ or part
league (لیگ) association, union	**lean** (لاغر) bend or slant away from the vertical, rely for assistance or support
leap (جهش) jump, hop, place jumped over or from	**legal** (مجاز) created by, permitted by law, according to the law of works
legendary (افسانهای) mythical, fabled, extremely well known, famous or renowned	**legitimate** (مشروع) accordant with law, lawful, based on logical reasoning, reasonable
lengthen (طولانی شدن) extend, make or become longer	**levy** (وضع مالیات) impose fine or tax, collect payment
liable (مسئولیت پذیر) bound or obliged in law or equity	**license** (مجوز) official or legal permission to do or own a specified thing
likelihood (احتمال) possibility, strong probability, state of being probable	**likewise** (به همین ترتیب) similarly, as well, too
limestone (سنگ آهک) rock consisting chiefly of calcium carbonate or carbonate of lime	**linear** (خطی) having form of a line, straight, consisting of lines, lineal
liner (بوش) vessel belonging to a regular line of packets, as ship or plane	**linger** (ماندن) be slow in leaving, continue or persist, stay
linguistics (زبانشناسی) humanistic study of language and literature	**liquid** (مایع) fluid, juice, substance in fluid state

list (لیست) lean or cause to lean to the side, lean over, itemize	**literal** (تحت اللفظی) according to the letter or verbal expression, exactly as stated
literate (باسواد) educated, schooled, one who can read and write	**litter** (آشغال) make untidy by discarding rubbish carelessly, scatter about
lively (زنده) busy, energetic, vigorous	**livestock** (دام) any animals kept for use or profit
loan (وام) give temporarily, temporary provision of money	**lobster** (خرچنگ) any large macrurous crustacean used as food
locality (محل) place, district, surrounding or nearby region, particular neighborhood	**locate** (پیدا کردن) find, monitor, settle, determine or specify the position or limits o
location (محل) scene, site, place where something is or could be located	**lodging** (اقامتگاه) accommodation, lodging
lofty (بلند) high, tall, having great height, idealistic, implying over-optimism	**log** (ورود به سیستم) record of a voyage or flight, record of day to day activities
logic (منطق) reasoned and reasonable judgment, a system of reasoning	**logical** (منطقی) reasonable, based on known statements or events or conditions
loom (متنفر) appear or take shape, usually in enlarged or distorted form	**loop** (حلقه) circle, ring, move in loops, make a loop in, join with a loop
loose (سست) unbound, untied, not attached, fastened, fixed, or confined	**loosen** (شل کنید) make loose or looser, make less severe or strict

lounge
(سالن)
public room with seating where people can wait, living room, lobby

low
(کم)
utter sound made by cattle, make a low noise

lubricate
(روغن کاری کنید)
make smooth or slippery

lumber
(چوب)
move heavily or clumsily, cut down timber of

luminous
(درخشان)
shining, emitting light, especially emitting self-generated light

lunar
(قمری)
pertaining to the moon, affecting the moon

luxurious
(مجلل)
rich and superior in quality, lavish

magic
(شعبده بازی)
any art that invokes supernatural powers

magician
(جادوگر)
one who performs magic tricks to amuse an audience, sorcerer, wizard

magistrate
(دادرس)
civil officer with power to administer and enforce law

magnificent
(باشکوه)
grand or noble in thought or deed, outstanding of its kind

magnitude
(اندازه)
extent, greatness of rank, size, or position

maize
(ذرت)
tall annual cereal grass bearing kernels on large ears

major
(عمده)
greater in number, quantity, or extent, more important

majority
(اکثریت)
greater number or part, a number more than half of the total

malady
(ناخوشایند)
disease, disorder, or ailment, unwholesome condition

manifest
(مانیفست)
clearly apparent to understanding, obvious

manifesto
(بیانیه)
public declaration of principles, statement of policy

mansion
(عمارت)
dwelling-house of the better class, a large or stately residence

manual
(کتابچه راهنمای)
guide book, hand-operated

manufacture
(ساخت)
make products by hand or machinery, make from raw materials

maple
(افرا)
tree of the genus acer, including about fifty species

marble
(سنگ مرمر)
hard crystalline metamorphic rock that takes a high polish

margin
(لبه)
border, rim, room

marginal
(حاشیه ای)
of or pertaining to a margin, written or printed in the margin

marine
(دریایی)
sea-dwelling, maritime, naval

marked
(مشخص شده است)
noticeable or pronounced, having one or more distinguishing marks

marsh
(باتلاق)
swamp, bog, low lying wet land with grassy vegetation

marshal
(مارشال)
put in order, arrange or place something in line

marvel
(شگفتی)
wonder, strong surprise, astonishment

masculine
(مردانه)
of the male sex, not female, having the qualities of a man

mask
(ماسک)
try to conceal something, disguise, hide under a false appearance

masterpiece
(شاهکار)
chief excellence or great talent, outstanding work of art or craft

match
(همخوانی داشتن)
something that resembles or harmonizes with

mate
(رفیق)
a fellow member of a team

materialism
(ماتریالیسم)
philosophical theory that matter is the only reality

mathematics
(ریاضیات)
science dealing with the logic of quantity and shape

mature
(بالغ)
develop and reach maturity, grow old or older

maximum
(بیشترین)
the largest possible quantity

mechanics
(مکانیک)
branch of physics concerned with the motion of bodies

mechanism (سازوکار) device, machine, the technical aspects of doing something	**medieval** (قرون وسطایی) very old-fashioned, as if belonging to the middle ages
medium (متوسط) state that is intermediate between extremes	**meek** (احمق) quiet and obedient, showing patience and humility
melancholy (مالیخولیا) gloomy, feeling of thoughtful sadness, affected by depression	**memo** (یادداشت) short note, memorandum, written proposal or reminder
memorize (حفظ کردن) commemorate, commit to memory, learn by heart	**mend** (بهبودی یافتن) make repairs or restoration to, fix, improve
mental (ذهنی) involving mind or intellectual process, affected by disorder of mind	**mentality** (ذهنیت) mental action or power, intellectual activity, intellectuality
mention (اشاره) speak or notice of anything, usually in a brief or cursory manner	**menu** (منو) an agenda of things to do
mercantile (بازرگان) trading, commercial, of or relating to trade or traders	**merchandise** (کالا) objects for sale, goods
merge (ادغام) combine, unite	**merit** (شایستگی) virtue, admirable quality or attribute, credit
metallic (فلزی) of or pertaining to metal, of metal nature, resembling metal	**method** (روش) orderly procedure or process, regular manner of doing anything
methodology (روش) system of methods followed in a particular discipline	**metropolitan** (شهر بزرگ) city center, one who lives in a city center

microscope (میکروسکوپ) magnifier of the image of small objects	**microwave** (مایکروویو) a short electromagnetic wave, cook or heat in a microwave oven
mighty (توانا) having or showing great strength or force or intensity	**migrate** (مهاجرت) move from one country or region to another and settle there
migration (مهاجرت) movement of persons from one country or locality to another	**milestone** (نقطه عطف) landmark, significant development
military (نظامی) pertaining to soldiers, to arms, or to war, of whole body of soldiers	**miller** (آسیاب) one who keeps or attends a flour mill or gristmill, milling machine
millionaire (میلیونر) one whose material wealth is valued at more than a million dollars	**miniature** (مینیاتوری) very small, model that represents something in a greatly reduced size
minimize (به حداقل رساندن) diminish, belittle, make small or insignificant	**minimum** (کمترین) the smallest possible quantity
minus (منهای) less, requiring to be subtracted, negative	**minute** (دقیقه) extremely small, short note
miracle (معجزه) wonderful thing, something that excites admiration or astonishment	**miraculous** (معجزه گر) astonishing, amazing
miserable (بدبخت) very unhappy, full of misery, wretched	**misery** (بدبختی) great unhappiness, extreme pain of body or mind
misfortune (بد شانسی) bad fortune or ill luck, bad luck	**mishap** (سوء استفاده) unfortunate accident, bad luck

mislead	**mobile**
(گمراه کردن)	(سیار)
deceive, misguide	movable, not fixed, fluid, unstable
mock	**mode**
(مسخره کردن)	(حالت)
treat with ridicule or contempt, mimic, frustrate hopes of	prevailing style, manner, way of doing something, fashion or style
moderate	**modest**
(در حد متوسط)	(فروتن)
temperate, gentle, mild, make less fast or intense , preside over	humble, less ambitious, moderate
modulate	**moist**
(مدوله کردن)	(مرطوب)
tone down in intensity, regulate, change from one key to another	slightly wet, damp or humid
moisture	**molecular**
(مرطوب)	(مولکولی)
wetness caused by water	of molecules, relating to simple or basic structure or form
momentary	**momentous**
(آنی)	(با اهمیت)
done in a moment, continuing only a moment, lasting a very short time	very important, of outstanding significance or consequence
monarch	**monetary**
(سلطنت)	(پولی)
king, sole and absolute ruler, sovereign, such as a king or empress	of or relating to money, nation's currency, financial
monopolize	**monopoly**
(انحصار)	(انحصار)
dominate, occupy, have and control fully and exclusively	exclusive control or possession of something, domination
monotonous	**monument**
(یکنواخت)	(بنای تاریخی)
boring, dull, tediously repetitious or lacking in variety	structure erected to commemorate persons or events, memorial
mortal	**motel**
(فانی)	(متل)
man, human being, liable or subject to death, accompanying death	motor hotel, lodging rooms adjacent to a parking lot

motion	**motivate**
(حرکت ـ جنبش)	(ایجاد انگیزه)
movement, act of changing location, ability or power to move	stimulate, impel, provide with an incentive, move to action
motto	**mould**
(شعار)	(قالب)
short, suggestive expression of a guiding principle, maxim	crumbling, soft, friable earth, soil
mount	**mourn**
(کوه)	(سوگواری)
go up or advance, fix onto a backing, put up or launch	express or to feel grief or sorrow, grieve, be sorrowful
mournful	**mourning**
(عزادار)	(عزاداری)
feeling or expressing sorrow or grief, sad, gloomy	expression of deep sorrow because someone has died
muffle	**multiple**
(صدا خفه کن)	(چندگانه)
bare end of nose between nostrils	having, or consisting of more than one part, many
multiply	**multitude**
(تکثیر کردن)	(جمع)
proliferate, increase, combine by multiplication	a great number, many
municipal	**murmur**
(شهرداری)	(زمزمه)
metropolitan, civic, having local self-government	make low, confused, and indistinct sound, like that of running water
muse	**mushroom**
(موزه)	(قارچ)
be absorbed in one's thoughts, consider or say thoughtfully	multiply, grow, or expand rapidly
mutton	**mutual**
(گوشت گوسفند)	(متقابل)
sheep, flesh of a sheep, loose woman, prostitute	common to or shared by two or more parties, shared
myriad	**mysterious**
(بی شمار)	(اسرار امیز)
of very large or indefinite number, of ten thousand	beyond ordinary understanding

myth (اسطوره) legend, fable, a traditional story accepted as history	**mythology** (اسطوره شناسی) study of myths, collection of myths
naked (برهنه) bare and pure, completely unclothed	**namely** (برای مثال) by name, by particular mention, expressly, that is to say
nap (چرت زدن) a period of time spent sleeping	**narrator** (راوی) someone who tells a story
nasty (زننده) very dirty, foul, disgusting, nauseous	**native** (بومی) being as origin, as found in nature in the elemental form
navigation (جهت یابی) guidance of ships or airplanes from place to place	**needy** (نیازمند) poor, indigent, being in need, impoverished
negative (منفی) adverse, involving disadvantage or harm, pessimistic	**neglect** (بی توجهی) disregard, ignore, pay little or no attention to
negligible (ناچیز) so small, trifling, or unimportant that it may be easily disregarded	**negotiation** (مذاکره) discussion intended to produce an agreement
nervous (عصبی) agitated, anxious	**neutral** (خنثی) impartial, not supporting one side over another
neutron (نوترون) elementary particle with 0 charge and mass about equal to a proton	**nickel** (نیکل) coin worth one twentieth of a dollar
noisy (پر سر و صدا) full of loud and nonmusical sounds, clamorous	**nonsense** (مزخرف) silliness, words or signs having no intelligible meaning

norm (هنجار) convention, standard, rule	**normally** (به طور معمول) usually, as a rule, regularly, according to a rule
notable (قابل توجه) worthy of note or notice, remarkable, important	**notably** (به ویژه) especially, in a notable manner, remarkably, particularly
note (توجه داشته باشید) observe carefully, notice, show, indicate	**notion** (ایده) general or universal conception, belief or opinion
notorious (بدنام) disreputable, known widely and usually unfavorably, infamous	**nourishment** (تغذیه) a source of materials to nourish the body
novel (رمان) previously unknown, strikingly new, unusual, or different, young	**novelty** (تازگی) quality of being novel, newness, something new and unusual
nowadays (این روزها) during current time, presently	**nowhere** (هیچ کجا) not anywhere, not in any place or state
null (خالی) invalid, void, nullified, having no legal force, invalid	**numerous** (بیشمار) many, various, amounting to a large indefinite number
nursery (مهد کودک) room for baby, area in a household set apart for the use of children	**nylon** (نایلون) any of a family of high-strength, resilient synthetic polymers
oath (سوگند ـ دشنام) solemn promise, commitment to tell the truth	**object** (هدف ـ شیی) be averse to or express disapproval of
objection (اعتراض) act of expressing earnest opposition or protest	**objective** (هدف، واقعگرایانه) not influenced by emotions, having actual existence or reality

obscure

(مبهم)

darken, make dim or indistinct, conceal in obscurity

obstacle

(مانع)

one that opposes, stands in the way of, or holds up progress

obstruction

(انسداد)

act of obstructing, any structure that makes progress difficult

obtain

(به دست آوردن)

get hold of, gain possession of, acquire, in any way

obtainable

(قابل دستیابی)

available, capable of being obtained

occasional

(گاه به گاه)

random, occurring from time to time, infrequent

occasionally

(گاه و بیگاه)

now and then, from time to time, infrequently, irregularly

occupy

(اشغال)

inhabit, live in a certain place, be present in, be inside of

occur

(به وقوع پیوستن)

take place, be found to exist , come to one's mind

occurrence

(وقوع)

an event that happens

odour

(بو)

any smell, whether fragrant or offensive, scent, perfume

offend

(توهین)

strike against, attack, assail, make angry, affront

offensive

(توهین آمیز)

causing anger, displeasure, resentment, or affront

offset

(انحراف)

counterbalance, counteract, or compensate for, balance

ominous

(شوم)

threatening, foreshadowing evil or tragic developments

onset

(شروع)

beginning or early stages, offensive against enemy

opera

(اپرا)

a drama set to music and consists of singing

opponent

(حریف)

contestant, someone who offers opposition , adverse, hostile, opposing

opportune

(فرصت طلب)

timely, just in time, suited or right for a particular purpose

opposition

(مخالفت)

condition of being in conflict, act of opposing something

optical (نورى) of or relating to or involving light or optics	**optimistic** (خوش بين) hopeful, positive, expecting the best in all possible ways
option (گزينه) act of choosing, power or freedom to choose	**optional** (اختيارى) not obligatory, left to choice, not compulsory or automatic
oral (دهانى) spoken, unwritten, relating to the mouth	**orbit** (مدار) path, circle, move in an orbit, encircle
orchard (باغچه) garden, area of land devoted to the cultivation of fruit or nut trees	**orderly** (منظم) conformed to order, in order, regular, well-regulated
ore (سنگ معدن) mineral that contains metal that is valuable enough to be mined	**organic** (ارگانيک. آلى) simple and healthful and close to nature
origin (اصل و نسب) the first existence or beginning of anything, birth, fountain	**original** (اصلى) not second hand, not copied or translated from something else
originality (اصالت) novelty, creativity, capacity to act or think independently	**originate** (سرچشمه) initiate, invent, bring into being, create
ornament (زينت) decoration, something used to beautify	**ornamental** (زينتى) decorative, any plant grown for its beauty or ornamental value
ounce (اونس) unit of weight equal to one sixteenth of a pound	**outbreak** (شيوع) beginning, eruption, explosion
outcome (نتيجه) result, end or consequence, result of a random trial	**outlook** (چشم انداز) prospect, view, belief about the future , act of looking out

outrage (خشم) act of extreme violence or viciousness, offense	**outright** (كاملا) altogether, entirely, without reservation or exception
outset (شروع) beginning, start, origin, time at which something is supposed to begin	**outstanding** (برجسته) distinguished from others in excellence
oval (بیضی) elliptic, rounded like an egg	**overcast** (پوشیده از ابر) covered or obscured, as with clouds or mist, gloomy, melancholy
overcharge (اضافه بار) overprice, a price that is too high	**overcome** (غلبه بر) defeat another in competition or conflict, conquer, prevail over
overestimate (زیاده روی کردن) make too high an estimate of	**overhear** (شنیدن) hear more of anything than was intended to be heard, hear again
overlapping (با هم تداخل دارند) covering with a design in which one element covers a part of another	**overload** (اضافه بار) place too much a load on
overseas (در خارج از کشور) beyond or across the sea, abroad	**owe** (مدیون) be in debt, be obliged to pay or repay
owl (جغد) any species of raptorial birds of the family strigidae	**own** (مال خود) belonging to oneself or itself, not foreign, domestic
ownership (مالکیت) having and controlling property	**oyster** (صدف خوراکی) marine mollusks having a rough irregular shell
pace (سرعت) single movement from one foot to the other in walking, slow gait, step	**packaging** (بسته بندی) putting something into boxes

pale
(کمرنگ)
not ruddy, dusky white, pallid, not bright or brilliant

pamphlet
(جزوه)
brochure, leaflet, a small book usually having a paper cover

pan
(ماهی تابه)
criticize harshly, wash in pan, cook in pan

panel
(تابلو)
a group of people gathered for a special purpose, small board or pad

panic
(وحشت)
sudden mass fear and anxiety

panorama
(پانوراما)
complete view in every direction.

pantry
(آبدارخانه)
apartment or closet in which bread and other provisions are kept

pants
(شلوار)
trousers, underwear, garment extending from waist to knee or ankle

parade
(رژه)
march in a procession, ceremonial procession, visible display

paradise
(بهشت)
garden of eden, any place of complete delight and peace

paralyse
(فلج کردن)
make unable to move or act, impair the progress or functioning of

parameter
(پارامتر)
characteristic or feature that distinguishes something from others

participant
(شرکت کننده)
people who take part in

participate
(مشارکت کردن)
take part in something, share in something

particle
(ذره)
a tiny piece of anything

partition
(تَقسیم بندی)
divide into parts, pieces, or sections

passion
(شور)
strong feeling or emotion , fervor

passionate
(پرشور)
zealous, enthusiastic, filled with or motivated by zeal

pasture
(مرتَع)
field covered with grass, meadow

patch
(پچ)
a piece of cloth, small area of ground covered by specific vegetation

patent (ثبت اختراع) open for the public to read, obvious, plain	**path** (مسیر) way, footway, course or track, route, passage
pathetic (تأسف‌بار ـ رقت انگیز) causing sadness, compassion, or pity	**patriot** (وطن پرست) one who loves and defends his or her country
patriotic (میهن پرست) inspired by love for one's country	**patron** (حامی) benefactor, regular customer
patronage (حمایت) sponsorship, support, state of being a sponsor	**peak** (اوج) summit, apex, maximum, prime
pebble (سنگریزه) small smooth rounded rock	**peculiar** (عجیب و غریب) special, characteristic, unusual, odd, bizarre
pedal (پدال) foot-operated lever used for actuating or controlling a mechanism	**pedestrian** (عابر پیاده) lacking wit or imagination, ordinary
peer (همتا) gaze, stare, look searchingly, company with	**pending** (انتظار) not yet decided or settled, awaiting conclusion or confirmation
penetrate (نفوذ) pierce, go through, permeate	**penetration** (نفوذ) act or process of penetrating, piercing, or entering
perception (ادراک) understanding, feeling, effect or product of perceiving	**perfection** (کمال) flawlessness, excellence, state of being without flaw or defect
perform (انجام دادن) carry through, bring to completion, achieve, accomplish, execute	**perfume** (عطر) pleasing, agreeable scent or odor

perimeter (محیط) outer boundary length, closed curve bounding a plane area	**period** (عادت زنانه) duration, continuance, term, end of something
periodic (تناوبی) repeated, recurring at intervals of time	**peripheral** (پیرامونی) located in outer boundary, unimportant, auxiliary
perish (هلاک شود) be destroyed, pass away, become nothing	**permanent** (دائمی) remaining without essential change
permission (اجازه) consent, approval to do something	**permissive** (مجاز) approving, tolerant, granting, not strict in discipline
permit (اجازه) consent to, give permission	**perpetual** (همیشگی) everlasting, continuing without interruption
perseverance (استقامت) endurance, steady persistence in adhering to a course of action	**persist** (اصرار ورزیدن) continue, insist, persevere
persistence (ماندگاری) endurance, tenacity, state or quality of being persistent, persistency	**personnel** (پرسنل) group of people willing to obey orders
perspective (چشم انداز) appearance of things, view, outlook, or vista	**persuade** (متقاعد کردن) advise, counsel, urge the acceptance or practice of, convince
pertinent (مرتبط) having precise or logical relevance, pertaining or relating	**pest** (آفت) persistently annoying person, organism that injures livestock or crops
pet (حیوان خانگی) animal kept for amusement or companionship	**petition** (دادخواست) plea, formal message requesting something

petroleum (نفت) dark oil consisting mainly of hydrocarbons	**petty** (خرده) trivial, of small importance, very small
phase (فاز) any distinct time period in a sequence of events, stage	**photograph** (عکس) picture or likeness obtained by photography
physical (جسمی) relating to the body as distinguished from the mind or spirit	**piano** (پیانو) stringed instrument that is played by depressing keys
picturesque (زیبا) scenic, striking or interesting in an unusual way	**pigment** (رنگدانه) substance used as coloring, dry coloring matter
pillow (بالش) a cushion to support the head of a sleeping person	**pine** (کاج) have desire for something or someone, yearn, grieve or mourn for
pineapple (آناناس) large sweet fleshy tropical fruit with a terminal tuft of stiff leaves	**pioneer** (پیشگام) originator, explorer
pioneering (پیشگام) initial, groundbreaking, originating, serving to pioneer	**pistol** (تپانچه) the smallest firearm used, intended to be fired from one hand
pit (گودال) confront, set into opposition or rivalry	**pitch** (گام صدا) action or manner of throwing something
plague (طاعون) epidemic disease with a high death rate, annoyance	**plane** (سطح) flat or level surface, level of development, existence, or achievement
planet (سیاره) celestial bodies that revolve around the sun	**plantation** (مزارع) farm, an area under cultivation, a group of cultivated trees or plants

plateau (فلات) highland, upland, relatively flat highland	**platform** (سکو) stage, a raised horizontal surface
playwright (نمایشنامه نویس) someone who writes plays	**plea** (رضای) request for help, excuse or pretext
plead (لابه کردن) appeal or request earnestly, enter a plea, offer as an excuse	**pledge** (سوگند ـ تعهد) promise solemnly and formally, binding commitment to do something
plight (گرفتاری) condition or state, especially a bad state or condition	**plot** (طرح) small extent of ground, secret scheme or strategy
plumb (پلمب) checking perpendicularity, exactly vertical	**plumber** (لوله کش) craftsman who installs and repairs pipes and fixtures and appliances
plump (چاق شدن) sound of a sudden heavy fall, well-rounded and full in form	**plunder** (غارت) take goods of by force, or without right, spoil, sack, strip, rob
pneumonia (ذات الریه) inflammation of the lungs	**polar** (قطبی) pertaining to one of the poles of the earth, of the poles
pole (قطب) a long rod, one of two divergent or mutually exclusive opinions	**polish** (لهستانی) remove flaws from, perfect or complete
poll (نظرسنجی) voting, survey, number of votes cast or recorded	**popcorn** (ذرت بو داده) small kernels of corn exploded by heat
popularity (محبوبیت) quality of being widely admired or accepted or sought after	**porcelain** (ظروف چینی) ceramic ware made of a more or less translucent ceramic

port
(بندر)
place on waterway with facilities for loading and unloading ships

portable
(قابل حمل)
mobile, easily or conveniently transported

portion
(بخش)
section or quantity within a larger thing, a part of a whole

positive
(مثبت)
involving advantage or good , greater than zero, very sure, confident

possession
(مالکیت)
act of having and controlling property, belongings

post
(پست)
display announcement in a place of public view, publish on a list

postage
(پستی)
token that postal fee has been paid, charge for mailing something

postal
(پستی)
of or relating to the system for delivering mail

postcard
(کارت پستال)
card for sending messages by post without an envelope

postpone
(عقب انداختن)
hold back to a later time, delay, defer

postulate
(فرضیه)
essential premise, underlying assumption

potential
(پتانسیل)
existing in possibility, expected to become or be

pound
(پوند)
unit of weight equal to 16 ounces

pour
(ریختن)
flow in a spurt, rain heavily, supply in large amounts

practicable
(عملی)
feasible, capable of being effected, done, or put into practice

practical
(کاربردی)
based on experience, useful

practically
(عملا)
virtually, actually, for all practical purpose

prairie
(دلفریب)
treeless grassy plain, extensive area of flat or rolling

preach
(موعظه)
advocate, speak, plead, argue in favor of

precaution
(احتیاط)
prevention, measure taken beforehand, act of foresight

preceding	precious
(قبل)	(گرانبها)
ahead, prior to	of high worth or cost

precise	predecessor
(دقیق)	(سلف، اسبق، جد)
exact, clearly expressed, accurate or correct	former occupant of post, ancestor or forefather

prediction	predominant
(پیش بینی)	(غالب)
something foretold or predicted, prophecy	most frequent or common, having superior power and influence

preferable	preference
(ارجح است)	(ترجیح)
favored, better, more desirable or worthy than another, preferred	a strong liking, favorite

pregnancy	preliminary
(بارداری)	(مقدماتی)
condition of being pregnant, fruitfulness, fertility	prior to or preparing for the main matter, introductory

prelude	premium
(مقدمه)	(حق بیمه)
introduction, forerunner, preliminary or preface	having or reflecting superior quality or value

prescribe	prescribed
(تجویز کنید)	(تجویز شده)
dictate, guide, advise the use of, assert a right, claim	set down as a rule or guide, certain, stated

presence	presentation
(حضور)	(ارائه)
state of being present, current existence	show or display, act of presenting something to sight or view

preservation	preserve
(حفظ)	(حفظ)
conservation, protection	uphold, retain, maintain in safety from injury, peril, or harm

pressure	pretense
(فشار)	(تظاهر)
stress, tension, condition of being pressed	act of giving a false appearance, imaginative intellectual play

prevailing (غالب) most frequent, widespread, predominant	**prevalent** (رواج دارد) widespread, widely or commonly occurring, existing, accepted
previous (قبلی) existing or occurring before something else	**prey** (طعمه) target of a hunt, animal hunted or caught for food
prick (لرزان) penetrate or puncture by a sharp and slender thing	**primary** (اولیه) of first rank or importance or value, essential or basic
primitive (اولیه) belonging to an early stage, simple or naive in style, primeval	**principal** (مدیر) highest in rank, authority, character, importance, or degree
prior (قبلی) preceding in the order of time, former, previous	**priority** (اولویت) preceding in time, importance, or urgency
probe (پویشگر) explore with tools, investigate, search	**problematic** (مشکل ساز) open to doubt, unsettled, questionable, difficult to solve
proceed (ادامه دهید) follow a certain course, move ahead, travel onward	**proceeding** (اقدام) a sequence of steps by which legal judgments are invoked
productivity (بهره وری) quality or state of being productive, productiveness.	**profession** (حرفه) occupation requiring special education
professional (حرفه ای) engaged in, or suitable for a profession	**proficient** (ماهر) skilled, expert, having or showing knowledge and skill and aptitude
profile (مشخصات) outline, biographical sketch	**profound** (ژرف) deep, not superficial, far-reaching

progress
(پیش رفتن)
moving or going forward, proceeding onward, advance

progressive
(ترقی خواه)
forward-looking, advancing, incremental

prohibit
(ممنوع کرده است)
ban, taboo, forbid

prohibitive
(گران، منع کننده)
tending to discourage, prohibiting, forbidding

proletarian
(پرولتاریایی)
member of working class, blue collar person

prolong
(طولانی شدن)
make longer, draw out, lengthen

prominent
(برجسته)
conspicuous, immediately noticeable, sticking out, widely known

promising
(امیدوار کننده)
likely to develop in a desirable manner, affording hope

prompt
(سریع)
move to act, incite, give rise to, assist with a reminder

propel
(سوق دادن)
drive forward, cause to move forward or onward, push

propeller
(پروانه)
machine for propelling an aircraft or boat, one who propels

property
(ویژگی)
any tangible or intangible possession that is owned by someone

proposal
(پیشنهاد)
something proposed, act of making a proposal, an offer of marriage

proprietor
(مالک)
one who has legal title to something, owner

prose
(پروسه)
essay, ordinary speech or writing, commonplace expression or quality

prospect
(چشم انداز)
possibility of future success, belief about future

prosperity
(سعادت)
good fortune, financial success, physical well-being

protest
(اعتراض)
expression of disagreement and disapproval, complain against

prototype
(نمونه اولیه)
original work used as a model, original type

provincial
(استانی)
relating to a province, limited in outlook, unsophisticated

provisional (موقت) temporary, provided for present need only	**provocation** (تحریک) unfriendly behavior that causes anger or resentment, aggravation
prudent (محتاط، معقول) cautious, careful in regard to one's own interests	**psychology** (روانشناسی) science that deals with mental processes and behavior
publish (انتشار) make public, make known to mankind, or to people in general	**pulse** (نبض) beat, rhythm, rate at which heart beats,
pump (پمپ) draw fluid or gas by pressure or suction, supply in great quantities	**pumpkin** (کدو تنبل) usually large pulpy deep-yellow round fruit of the squash family
punch (پانچ) blow, drive forcibly, pierce, hit with a sharp blow of the fist	**punctual** (وقت شناس) consisting in a point, limited to a point, unexpended, precise
pupil (شاگرد) a learner who is enrolled in an educational institution	**puppy** (توله سگ) young dog, pup, doll, puppet
pursue (دنبال کردن) follow in, go in search of or hunt for	**pursuit** (دستیابی) follow after, follow with a view to obtain, endeavor to attain
puzzle (پازل) difficult question or problem	**qualification** (صلاحیت) an attribute that must be met
qualitative (کیفی) relating to quality, having the character of quality	**quarterly** (سه ماه یکبار) every three months, in three month intervals
quartz (کوارتز) a hard glossy mineral consisting of silicon dioxide in crystal form	**quench** (فرو نشاندن) put out a fire, extinguish, put an end to, destroy

quest
(جستجو)
act of searching for something

quilt
(لحاف)
bedding made of two layers of cloth filled with stuffing

quiver
(لرزیدن)
shake with slight, rapid, tremulous movement

quota
(سهمیه، سهم)
limitation on imports, ration, prescribed number

quote
(نقل قول)
cite or repeat a passage from, repeat or copy the words of another

rack
(دندانه دار کردن)
framework for holding objects

radar
(رادار)
measuring instrument to detect distant objects by microwave

radiant
(تابشی)
brilliant, delighted

radiate
(تابش)
spread out, effuse, issue or emerge in rays or waves

radical
(افراطی)
drastic, extreme, arising from or going to a root or source, basic

rage
(خشم)
something that is desired intensely, state of extreme anger

raid
(حمله)
search without warning, surprise attack by a small armed force

rally
(تظاهرات)
call up or summon, call together for a common purpose

random
(تصادفی)
without definite purpose, plan, or aim, having no specific pattern

rare
(نادر)
scarce, infrequently occurring, uncommon

rarely
(به ندرت)
not often, in an unusual degree, exceptionally

rat
(موش)
any of various long tailed rodents, similar to but larger than mouse

ratify
(تصویب)
approve formally, confirm, verify

ration
(جیره)
allotment, allowance, portion, allot, distribute in rations

rational
(گویا)
consistent with, based on, using reason

rattle
(لرزاندن)
a rapid series of short loud sounds, loosely connected horny sections

ravage
(ویرانی)
bring heavy destruction on, devastate

react
(واکنش نشان می دهند)
act against or in opposition to, show a response or a reaction

reactionary
(ارتجاعی)
opposition to progress or liberalism, extremely conservative

readily
(به راحتی)
easily, quickly, in a prompt, timely manner, promptly

realm
(قلمرو)
kingdom, domain ruled by a king or queen

reap
(درو کنید)
gain, harvest a crop from, get or derive, obtain as a result of effort

reassure
(اطمینان)
give or restore confidence in, cause to feel sure or certain

rebellion
(شورش)
organized opposition to authority

rebuke
(توبه کردن)
scold harshly, criticize severely

recall
(به خاطر آوردن)
remember, call back, cause to be returned

recede
(عقب نشینی)
move back, retreat, withdraw a claim or pretension

receipt
(اعلام وصول)
act of receiving, acknowledgment of goods delivered or money paid

reception
(پذیرایی)
act of receiving, manner in which something is greeted

recession
(رکود اقتصادی)
withdrawal, retreat, time of low economic activity

recipient
(گیرنده)
receiver, one that receives or is receptive

reckless
(بی پروا)
headstrong, rash, indifferent to or disregardful of consequences

recognition
(به رسمیت شناختن)
acceptance , appreciation, approval

recollection
(یادآوری)
memory, remembrance, power of recalling ideas to the mind

recommend
(توصیه)
suggest, bestow commendation on, represent favorably

recommendation (توصیه) making attractive or acceptable, pushing for something	**reconnaissance** (شناسایی) gain information about enemy, inspection or exploration of an area
recover (بازیابی) get or find back, regain a former condition	**recreation** (تفریح) amusement, entertainment
recurrence (عود) act of recurring, or state of being recurrent, return	**reed** (نی) tall woody perennial grasses with hollow slender stems
reef (تپه دریایی) chain or range of rocks lying at or near the surface of the water	**referee** (داور) someone to investigate and report on a case or to ensure fair play
refine (پالودن) purify, make more precise, improve	**refined** (تصفیه شده) cultured, purified, made pure
refinement (اصلاح) result of improving something, process of removing impurities	**refrain** (خودداری) abstain from, resist, hold oneself back
refrigerator (یخچال و فریزر) machines in which food can be stored at low temperatures	**refugee** (پناهنده) one who flees to shelter, or place of safety
refund (بازپرداخت) repayment of fund, an amount repaid	**refusal** (امتناع) act of refusing, denial of anything demanded
refute (رد کردن) disprove, prove to be false or incorrect	**regarding** (با توجه) with respect to, by concerning
regardless (بدون در نظر گرفتن) without consideration, in spite of everything, anyway	**regiment** (هنگ) government, mode of ruling, rule, authority

register
(ثبت نام)
give outward signs of, express, record in writing, enroll as a student

rehearse
(تمرین کردن)
practice, drill, engage in preparation for a public performance

reign
(سلطنت کن)
sovereignty, rule, dominance or widespread influence

reimburse
(بازپرداخت)
pay back for some expense incurred

reinforce
(تقویت)
give more force or effectiveness to, strengthen, enhance

reiterate
(تکرار کنید)
say, state, or perform again or repeatedly

reject
(رد کردن)
turn down, refuse to accept, dismiss from consideration

rejection
(طرد شدن)
act of rejecting something

relax
(آروم باش)
make less severe or strict, become less tense

relaxation
(آرامش)
state of refreshing tranquility, act of making less strict

release
(رهایی)
give off, liberate, grant freedom to, make something available

relevant
(مربوط)
pertinent, having connection with matter at hand

reliability
(قابلیت اطمینان)
trait of being dependable or reliable

reliable
(قابل اعتماد)
worthy of being depended on, trustworthy

reliance
(تکیه)
dependence, certainty based on past experience

relieve
(از بین بردن)
free from a burden, alleviate, save from ruin

relinquish
(انصراف دادن)
give up something with reluctance, retire from, give up or abandon

reluctant
(بی میل)
not wanting to take some action, averse

rely
(تکیه)
rest with confidence, have confidence, depend

remainder
(باقیمانده)
remnant, something left after other parts have been taken away

remark (تذكر) expression, in speech or writing, of something remarked or noticed	**remarkable** (قابل توجه) worthy of notice, extraordinary
remedy (اصلاح) a medicine or therapy, , cure, fix, repair, provide relief for	**remind** (به یاد آوردن) recall knowledge from memory, have a recollection
reminiscence (یادآوری) recollection, process of remembering	**renaissance** (رنسانس) revival, renewal, revival of learning and culture
renew (تجدید) renovate, make new or as if new again, restore	**renewable** (تجدید پذیر) capable of being renewed or extended
renewal (بازسازی) act of renewing, filling again by supplying what has been used up	**rent** (اجاره دادن) payment, usually of an amount fixed by contract
rental (اجاره ای) amount paid or collected as rent, act of renting	**repel** (دفع) force or drive back, disgust, offer resistance to, fight against
repent (توبه کردن) cause to feel remorse or regret, feel regret or self-reproach for	**repetition** (تکرار) act of doing or performing again
replenish (دوباره پر کردن) fill or make complete again, add a new stock or supply to	**represent** (نمایندگی) stand for, describe or present, play a role or part
reproach (سرزنش) express disapproval or disappointment, bring shame upon, disgrace	**reproduce** (تکثیر) have offspring or young, duplicate, make a copy
reproduction (تولید مثل) act of making copies	**repudiate** (رد کردن) disown, refuse to acknowledge, reject validity or authority of

reputable (معتبر) having a good reputation, honorable	**repute** (شهرت) ascribe a particular fact or characteristic to, consider, suppose
request (درخواست) express the need or desire for, ask for	**require** (نیاز) insist upon having, request and expect
requisite (مورد نیاز) necessary requirement, indispensable item	**rescue** (نجات) free from harm or evil, take from legal custody by force
research (پژوهش) inquire into, attempt to find out in scientific manner	**resemblance** (شباهت) likeness, similarity in appearance or external or superficial details
resent (خشم) feel bitter, consider as injury or affront, be in angry	**resentment** (نارضایتی) indignation, deep sense of injury, strong displeasure
reside (اقامت داشتن) dwell, live in a place permanently or for an extended period	**residence** (محل اقامت) official house, large house, act of dwelling in a place
residual (باقیمانده) remaining as a residue, surplus	**resign** (استعفا دهید) sign back, return by a formal act, yield to another, abandon
resistance (مقاومت) action of opposing something that you disapprove or disagree with	**resistant** (مقاوم) unaffected, incapable of being affected
resolve (برطرف کردن) determination, formal expression by a meeting, agreed to by a vote	**resort** (رفت و آمد مکرر) vacation spot, act of turning to for assistance
resource (منبع) materials, abilities, available source	**respect** (توجه) honor or esteem, admire, aspect, detail or point

respond (پاسخ دادن) show a reaction to something favorably or as hoped	**responsible** (مسئول) accountable, held accountable
restore (بازگرداندن) give or bring back, return to its original condition	**restrain** (مهار کردن) keep under control, hold back , place limits on
restrict (محدود کردن) keep or confine within limits	**restrictive** (محدود کننده) tending or serving to restrict, limiting, confining
resume (از سرگیری) give a summary, return to a previous location or condition	**retail** (خرده فروشی) selling of goods to consumers
retroactive (برگشت پذیر) extending in scope or effect to a prior time or to prior conditions	**reveal** (فاش کردن) make known, disclose or show
revenge (انتقام) do punishment in return for injury or insult, avenge	**revenue** (درآمد) money which returns from an investment, annual income, reward
revision (تجدید نظر) modification, correction, act of altering	**revival** (احیای) bringing again into activity and prominence
revive (احیای) restore from a depressed, renew	**revoke** (لغو) void or annul by recalling, withdrawing, or reversing, cancel, retract
revolt (شورش) organize opposition to authority, make revolution	**revolutionary** (انقلابی) marked by new or introducing radical change
rhythm (ریتم) pattern, beat, recurring at regular intervals	**riddle** (معما) pierce with numerous holes, perforate, permeate or spread throughout

ridge (خط الراس) long, narrow upper section or crest, chain of hills or mountains	**ridicule** (تمسخر) words or actions intended to evoke contemptuous laughter, make fun of
ridiculous (مسخره ـ مضحک) completely lacking of wisdom or good sense	**rifle** (تفنگ) shoulder firearm with a long barrel
righteous (عادل) morally justified, equitable, free from wrong, guilt, or sin	**rigid** (سفت و سخت) stiff and unyielding, strict, hard and unbending, not flexible
rigidity (سختی) stiffness, physical property of being stiff and resisting bending	**rigorous** (سختگیرانه) full of rigors, harsh, rigidly accurate, precise
rinse (شستشو) cleanse with water, flush, wash lightly without soap	**riot** (شورش) state of disorder involving group violence, rebellion
ripe (رسیده) ready, fully developed, mature	**ripen** (رسیدن) grow ripe, cause to ripen or develop fully
risky (خطرناک) involving risk or danger, hazardous	**rival** (رقیب) compete, be equal to in quality or ability, match
rivalry (رقابت) competition, the act of competing as for profit or a prize	**roam** (پرسه زدن) wander, ramble, stroll
robust (قدرتمند) vigorous, full of health and strength, vigorous	**rod** (میله) stick, a long thin implement made of metal or wood
roll (رول) a list of names	**rooster** (خروس) adult male chicken

rot (پوسیدگی) become decomposed by a natural process, perish slowly, become corrupt	**rotation** (چرخش) revolution, act of rotating as if on an axis
rough (خشن) not perfected, having or caused by an irregular surface	**roughly** (تَقریباً) approximately, more or less
route (مسیر) way for travel or transportation	**ruin** (خراب کردن) fall or tumble down, destroy, devastate, exterminate
ruinous (ویرانگر) causing, or tending to cause ruin, destructive, baneful, pernicious	**rural** (روستایی) country, relating to rural areas
rust (زنگ) become destroyed by water, air, or an etching chemical such as an acid	**ruthless** (بی رحمانه) pitiless, cruel, having no compassion or pity, merciless
sacred (مقدس) concerned with religion, worthy of respect or dedication	**saddle** (زین اسب) load or burden, put harness onto animal's back to ride
sake (منظور) purpose, reason for wanting something done	**sample** (نمونه) small part of something intended as representative of the whole
sandy (شنی) loose and large-grained in consistency	**sarcastic** (طعنه آمیز) ironic, expressing or expressive of ridicule that wounds
satellite (ماهواره) small body revolving around a larger one, subordinate	**save** (صرفه جویی) rescue, preserve, make unnecessary, set aside for future use
savings (پس انداز) resources, money saved	**scan** (اسکن) make a wide, sweeping search of, examine

scar (جای زخم) mark of damage, mark left on the skin after injury	**scarce** (کمبود) hard to find, absent or rare, limited
scarcely (به ندرت) hardly, barely, only just	**scare** (ترساندن) frighten, alarm, strike with sudden fear
scarf (روسری) long piece of cloth worn about the head, neck, or shoulders	**scarlet** (روسری) bright red
scent (بو) distinctive odor that is pleasant, fragrance, perfume	**schedule** (برنامه) plan for an activity or event, arrange
scholar (محقق) professor, a learned person	**scissors** (قیچی) edge tool having two crossed pivoting blades
scope (محدوده) range of one's perceptions, thoughts, or actions, extent, bound	**scotch** (اسکاچ) put an abrupt end to, block to prevent rolling or slipping
scrap (باطله) small piece or bit, fragment, fragment, leftover bits of food, remnant	**scrape** (خراشیدن) gather something together over time, scratch repeatedly
scratch (خراشیدن) cut the surface of, cause friction	**screen** (صفحه نمایش) surface where pictures can be projected for viewing , examine, test
screwdriver (پیچ گوشتی) a hand tool for driving screws	**script** (فیلمنامه) prepare text for filming or broadcasting
scrub (اسکراب) rub hard, wash with rubbing	**sculptor** (مجسمه ساز) artist who creates sculptures

sculpture (مجسمه سازی) statue, creating figures or designs in three dimensions	**seal** (مهر) middle size aquatic mammal, stamp used for authentication or security
seaport (بندر) sheltered port where ships can take on or discharge cargo	**seashore** (ساحل) coast, beach, the shore of a sea or ocean
seasonal (فصلی) occurring at or dependent on a particular season	**secret** (راز) something studiously concealed, a thing kept from general knowledge
secure (امن است) free from fear, care, or anxiety, not have reason to doubt	**security** (امنیت) freedom from risk or danger, safety
seek (جستجو کردن) make an effort to, try to get, try to discover	**seemingly** (ظاهرا) apparently, supposedly
segment (بخش) sector, portion, any of the parts into which something can be divided	**selection** (انتخاب) choice, variety, collection
sensational (احساسی) arousing or intended to arouse strong curiosity, interest, or reaction	**sentimental** (احساساتی) emotional, resulting from emotion rather than reason or realism
separate (جداگانه، مجزا) set or keep apart, disunite, divide, disconnect	**serene** (بی سر و صدا) completely clear and fine
serenity (آرامش) calmness of mind, quietness, stillness, peace	**series** (سلسله) a number of things or events standing or succeeding in order, sequence
setting (تنظیمات) context and environment in which something is set	**severe** (شدید) serious in feeling or manner, not light, lively, or cheerful

shabby (شاد) torn or worn to rage, poor, mean, ragged	**shallow** (کم عمق) lacking physical depth, not deep or strong
sham (شام) pretend, put on false appearance of, feign	**sharpen** (تیز کردن) make pointed, make sharp or sharper
sharply (به شدت) steeply, changing suddenly in direction and degree, acutely	**shatter** (خرد کردن) destroy, break up, break into many pieces
shave (تراشیدن) act of removing hair with a razor, thin slice or scraping	**shear** (برش) cut or clip hair, strip of something, remove by cutting or clipping
shed (دهنه) get rid of , cast off, cause to pour forth	**sheer** (خالص، ناب) very thin or transparent, very steep, absolute or pure
shelter (پناه) structure that provides privacy and protection from danger	**shepherd** (شبان) a herder of sheep, someone who keeps the sheep together in a flock
shield (سپر) protective covering or structure, protect, guard	**shift** (تغییر مکان) moving from one setting or context to another, moving very slightly
shiny (براق) reflecting light, radiant, bright from reflected light	**shipment** (حمل و نقل) sending of cargo, act of sending off something
shortcut (میانبر) a direct route, a route shorter than the usual one	**shot** (شلیک کرد) photographic view or exposure
shrewd (زیرک) clever, characterized by keen awareness, sharp intelligence	**shroud** (کفن) hide from view, wrap for burial, shut off from sight, shelter

shun	shutter
(اجتناب کردن)	(کرکره)
avoid deliberately, keep away from	a hinged blind for a window

shy	sick
(حجالتی)	(بیمار)
timid, bashful, easily startled, distrustful	affected with disease of any kind, ill, indisposed, not in health

sickness	sideways
(بیماری)	(پهلو)
state that precedes vomiting, disease	with the side forward, to or from a side

sign	signal
(امضاء کردن)	(علامت)
public display of message, visible mark or indication	a sign made for the purpose of giving notice to a person

signature	significance
(امضا)	(اهمیت)
name written in own handwriting	message that is intended or expressed or signified, meaning

significant	signify
(قابل توجه)	(نشان دادن)
fairly large, important in effect or meaning	denote, mean, indicate

silly	simulate
(احمقانه)	(شبیه سازی)
exhibiting a lack of wisdom or good sense, foolish, stupid	make a pretence of, reproduce someone's behavior or looks

simultaneous	single
(همزمان)	(تنها)
existing, happening, or done at the same time	one only, consisting of one alone, alone, having no companion

singular	site
(مفرد)	(سایت)
unique, extraordinary, being only one	physical position in relation to the surroundings, position, location

sketch	skip
(طرح)	(جست و خیز)
draw or describe briefly, give the main points, summary of	jump lightly, hop, bypass

skirmish (تکان خوردن) minor battle in war, minor or preliminary conflict or dispute	**skull** (جمجمه) bony skeleton of the head of vertebrates
skyscraper (آسمان خراش) very tall building with many stories	**slam** (سیلی زدن) shut with force and a loud noise, strike with force
slander (تهمت) defamation, false and malicious statement or report about someone	**slap** (سیلی زدن) sharp blow from a flat object as an open hand, smack, sharp insult
slender (بلند بلند) having little width in proportion to height or length, long and thin	**slight** (جزئی) almost no, very little, deliberate discourtesy
slightly (اندکی) a little, a bit	**slim** (باریک) small in quantity, being of delicate or slender build
slip (لیز خوردن) move smoothly and easily, move out of position, move stealthily	**slippery** (لغزنده) smooth, being such as to cause things to slip or slide
slit (شکاف) long, straight, narrow cut or opening, slot, pocket	**slogan** (شعار) phrase used repeatedly, as in advertising or promotion
slope (شیب) be at an angle, incline, gradient	**slum** (زاغه) a district of a city marked by poverty and inferior living conditions
slumber (چرت) sleep, state of inactivity or dormancy	**smart** (هوشمندانه) clever, intelligent, showing mental alertness and calculation
smash (درهم کوبیدن) break in pieces by violence, dash to pieces, crush	**smooth** (صاف) free from obstructions, make surface shine

smoothly (به نرمی) in a smooth manner, successfully, easily	**snack** (خوراک مختصر) eat light informal meal, eat lightly
snatch (ربودن) grasp or seize hastily, eagerly, or suddenly	**snobbish** (خرابکاری) of or pertaining to a snob, vulgarly pretentious
soil (خاک) material in the surface of the earth	**solar** (خورشیدی) of or relating to the sun
solely (فقط) alone, only, without another	**solemn** (تشریفات) serious, somber, deeply earnest, serious, and sober
solitude (تنهایی) state of being alone, seclusion, lonely or secluded place	**solution** (راه حل) method for solving a problem, successful action of solving a problem
solvent (حلال) able to pay all debts, capable of meeting financial obligations	**somehow** (به نحوی) in one way or another, in some way not yet known, by some means
somewhat (قدری) to some extent or degree, rather, a bit, slightly	**soothe** (تسکین می یابد) cause to feel better, give moral or emotional strength to
sophisticated (پیچیده) wide-ranging knowledge, complex, intellectually appealing	**sophistication** (پختگی) being expert or having knowledge of some technical subject
sort (مرتب سازی) kind or species, a class of,	**sound** (صدا) sensation perceived by the ear, distinctive noise, long narrow inlet
sour (ترش) taste experience when vinegar or lemon juice, showing ill humor	**souvenir** (سوغات) token of remembrance, memento, something of sentimental value

sovereign
(پادشاه)
having supreme rank or power, self governing, excellent, independent

sow
(بذر)
plant, place seeds in or on

soy
(سویا)
soybean, most highly protein vegetable

spacecraft
(فضاپیما)
a vehicle for travelling in space

spacious
(بزرگ جادار فراخ)
wide, generous or large in area or extent, sizable

spark
(جرقه)
flash, sparkle, emit or produce sparks

spatial
(فضایی)
relating to space, existing in or connected with space

specialized
(تخصصی)
developed or designed for a special activity or function

species
(گونه ها)
a specific kind of something

specific
(خاص)
stated explicitly or in detail, definite

specify
(مشخص نمودن)
detail, designate

specimen
(نمونه)
model, sample, an example regarded as typical of its class

spectacle
(دیدنی)
demonstration, show

spectator
(تماشاگر)
observer, audience, one who looks on

speedy
(سریع)
fast, rapid, accomplished or arrived at without delay, prompt

spell
(هجی کردن)
name or write in order the letters constituting, add up to, signify

sphere
(کره)
ball, globe, a particular aspect of life or activity

spill
(ریختن)
pour, sudden drop from an upright position, flow or run out

spin
(چرخش)
turn round rapidly, move round rapidly, move swiftly

spiral
(مارپیچ)
rotary, curled, moving in a zigzag course, moving in shape of a coil

spiritual (معنوی) not tangible or material, belonging to religion, sacred, supernatural	**spit** (تف انداختن) expel or eject from the mouth, rain gently
splendid (پر زرق و برق) shining, very bright, magnificent, brilliant	**split** (شکاف) break apart, cut, devide
spoil (از بین بردن) go bad, rot, decay, become unfit for consumption or use	**spokesman** (سخنگو) man who speaks on behalf of another or others
spoon (قاشق) a piece of cutlery with a shallow bowl-shaped container and a handle	**spot** (نقطه) location, place, site, pinpoint, mark to allow easy recognition
spray (افشانه) a quantity of small objects flying through air	**spring** (بهار) develop suddenly, jump, move forward by leaps and bounds
sprout (جوانه) have new growth of a plant such as a new branch or a bud, shoot up	**squat** (چمباتمه زدن) stocky, short and thick, low and broad
squirrel (سنجاب) a kind of arboreal rodent having a long bushy tail	**stab** (چاقو) pierce with a pointed weapon, wound or kill by pointed instrument
stability (ثبات) balance, constancy	**stable** (پایدار) not easily moved or disturbed
stack (پشته) an orderly pile, heap, a large number , arrange in pile	**staff** (کارمندان) personnel who assist superior to carry out assigned task
stagger (مبهوت) sway, walk as if unable to control one's movements	**staircase** (راه پله) a way of access consisting of a set of steps

stale
(کهنه)

having lost freshness, lacking originality or spontaneity

stall
(غرفه)

small area set off by walls for special use, booth

standard
(استاندارد)

criteria, basis for comparison

standing
(ایستاده)

high reputation, esteem, maintaining an erect position

standpoint
(دیدگاه)

a mental position from which things are viewed

startle
(وحشت زده شدن)

move suddenly, or be excited, excite by sudden alarm, surprise

starvation
(گرسنگی)

act of depriving of food or subjecting to famine

starve
(گرسنگی)

hunger, deprive of food

static
(ایستا)

having no motion, being at rest, fixed, stationary

stationary
(ثابت)

fixed, immobile, static, not capable of being moved

statue
(مجسمه)

sculpture representing a human or animal

status
(وضعیت)

position relative to others, standing

statute
(اساسنامه)

law enacted by legislature, decree or edict, as of a ruler

steady
(ثابت)

securely in position, not shaky, not easily excited

steak
(استیک)

slice of meat, typically beef, usually cut thick

steep
(شیب تند)

soak, make thoroughly wet

stem
(ساقه)

stop flow of a liquid, make headway against

stereo
(استریو)

stereophonic sound-reproduction system

sterling
(استرلینگ)

any english coin of standard value, coined money

stern
(سخت)

hard, harsh, or severe in manner or character, firm or unyielding

stick (چوب) fasten into place by fixing an end, be a follower or supporter	**sticky** (چسبنده) glutinous, adhesive, covered with an adhesive agent, humid, stiff
stiff (سفت) not moving or operating freely, lacking ease in bending, resistant	**stimulation** (تحریک) arousing an organism to action
stink (بد بو) strong, offensive smell, disgusting odor, stench	**stipulation** (تصریح) provision, an agreement made by parties in a judicial proceeding
stitch (کوک) sew, knit, fasten or join with or as if with thread	**stoop** (قدم زدن) bend forward and down from the waist or the middle of the back
storey (طبقه) story, floor or level of a building or ship	**strait** (تنگه) difficult, stressful, narrow, not broad, tight, close, closely fitting
strap (بند) belt, band that goes over the shoulder and supports a garment or bag	**streak** (خط) a line or long mark of a different color from the ground, stripe, vein
strengthen (تَقویت) reinforce, fortify, make strong or increase the strength of	**stretch** (کش آمدن) extend, pull in opposite directions, lie down comfortably
stride (گام های بلند برداشتن) step, pace, significant progress	**strip** (نوار) remove the surface from
stripe (نوار) a kind or category, band, ribbon	**strive** (تلاش کن) endeavor, struggle or fight forcefully, exert much effort or energy
stroll (قدم زدن) wander on foot, ramble idly or leisurely	**structural** (ساختاری) of structure, affecting structure, constructional

structure	studio
(ساختار)	(استودیو)
complex construction or entity, complex composition of knowledge	workplace for the teaching or practice of an art

stuff	stuffy
(چیز)	(کثیف)
unspecified objects, tangible substance	stout, lacking sufficient ventilation, close, dull and boring

stumble	sturdy
(تلو تلو خوردن)	(محکم)
miss a step and fall or nearly fall, walk unsteadily	robust, strong, substantially made or constructed

style	subject
(سبک)	(موضوع)
particular kind, a way of expressing something	something to be treated, course or area of study

submit	subordinate
(ارسال)	(تابع)
refer for judgment or consideration, hand in, present	occupying lower rank, inferior, submissive

subsequent	subsequently
(متعاقب)	(متعاقبا)
following in time or order, succeeding, later	in a subsequent manner, at a later time, accordingly, therefore

substantiate	substitute
(اثبات)	(جایگزین)
establish by evidence, make firm or solid, support	exchange, put in the place of another

subtle	subtract
(نامحسوس)	(تفریق کردن)
slight, be difficult to detect or grasp by the mind	remove a part from the whole

subtraction	suburb
(منها کردن)	(حومه شهر)
reduction, deduction, removing a part from the whole	outskirts, usually residential area or community outlying a city

suck	sufficient
(مکیدن)	(کافی)
draw liquid into mouth, take in, draw something by vacuum	adequate, enough, being as much as is needed

suit (کت و شلوار) meet the requirements of, fit, please, satisfy	**suitable** (مناسب) appropriate to a purpose or an occasion
suitcase (چمدان) portable rectangular traveling bag for carrying clothes	**sullen** (طعنه دار) lonely, solitary, desolate, gloomy, dismal, affected with ill humor
sultry (شرجی) burning hot, extremely and unpleasantly hot	**summary** (خلاصه) brief statement that presents the main points
summon (احضار) call, bid, or cite, notify to come to appear, call upon to surrender	**sunlight** (نور خورشید) rays of the sun
sunrise (طلوع خورشید) daily event of the sun rising above the horizon	**sunset** (غروب خورشید) daily event of the sun sinking below the horizon
sunshine (آفتاب) moderate weather, suitable for outdoor activities, the rays of the sun	**superb** (عالی) of unusually high quality, excellent, wonderful
superficial (سطحی) trivial, of little substance, involving a surface only	**superior** (برتر) greater rank or station or quality, excellent
supervision (نظارت) management by overseeing the performance	**supplement** (مکمل) add as something seems insufficient, complement, extension, addition
supplementary (مکمل) added to complete or make up a deficiency	**suppose** (فرض کنید) imagine or admit to exist, assume to be true, believe, receive as true
suppress (سرکوب) put down by force or authority, overwhelm, keep from being revealed	**supreme** (عالی) most outstanding, highest, superior

surcharge (اضافی) an additional charge, charge an extra fee	**surge** (افزایش) outburst, roll or be tossed about on waves, as a boat
surgeon (جراح) one who performs manual operations on a patient	**surmise** (حدس و گمان) guess, infer something without sufficiently conclusive evidence
surpass (پیشی گرفتن) be or go beyond, as in degree or quality, exceed	**surrender** (تسلیم شدن) hand over, give up, give something into another's control
survey (نظر سنجی) poll, detailed critical inspection	**survival** (بقا) existence, remaining alive
survive (زنده ماندن) continue to live, endure or last	**survivor** (باز مانده) one who outlives another, one who lives through affliction
suspect (مشکوک) have doubts about, distrust	**suspend** (تعلیق) hang freely, postpone, delay
suspense (تعلیق) uncertain cognitive state, uncertainty	**suspicious** (مشکوک) openly distrustful and unwilling to confide, questionable
swallow (بلع) take back what one has said , enclose or envelop completely	**swarm** (ازدحام) dense moving crowd, large group of honeybees
swear (سوگند) affirm or utter a solemn declaration, make promise or resolve on oath	**sweater** (ژاکت) knitted garment covering the upper part of the body
sweep (جارو کردن) movement in an arc, clean with a broom, wide scope, winning all	**swift** (سریع) quick, moving or capable of moving with great speed

syllable
(هجا)

a unit of spoken language larger than a phoneme

symbol
(سمبل)

sign, something visible to represent something else invisible

symbolize
(سمبل کردن)

represent, signify, stand for

symmetry
(تَقارن)

arrangement of parts so that balance is obtained, congruity

sympathize
(همدردی کردن)

be understanding of, feel or express sympathy or compassion

sympathy
(ابراز همدردی)

compassion, pity, concern

synonym
(هم معنی)

two words that can be interchanged in a context

system
(سیستم)

organized structure for arranging or classifying

systematic
(نظام)

ordered, methodical, carried on using step-by-step procedures

tack
(تکل)

small, short, sharp-pointed nail, usually having a broad, flat head

tactics
(تاکتیکها)

strategy, policy, plan for attaining a particular goal

tag
(برچسب زدن)

attach, append, provide with a name or nickname, label

tailor
(خیاط)

one whose occupation is making garments, create clothes with cloth

talent
(استعداد)

skill, gift, marked innate ability, as for artistic accomplishment

tally
(رسم)

record by making a mark, reckon or count, keep score

tap
(ضربه زدن)

draw upon, strike lightly, make good use of

target
(هدف)

reference point to shoot at, goal intended to be attained

tariff
(تعرفه)

tax on goods coming into a country

task
(وظیفه)

labor or study imposed by another, undertake, labor

taste
(طعم)

have experience or enjoyment, take a sample of, have flavor

tease
(اذیت کردن)

tear into pieces, raise the fibers of

technician
(تکنسین)

one skilled particularly in the technical details of work

technique
(تکنیک)

practical method or art applied to some particular task, skillfulness

telegraph
(تلگراف)

apparatus used to communicate at a distance over a wire

telescope
(تلسکوپ)

a magnifier of images of distant objects

temporary
(موقت)

not permanent, not lasting

tempt
(دچار وسوسه کردن)

give rise to a desire by being attractive

temptation
(وسوسه)

act of tempting, or enticing to evil, seduction

tenant
(مستاجر)

occupant, one that pays rent to use land or building

tendency
(گرایش)

trend, a general direction in which something tends to move

tender
(مناقصه)

offer formally, extend, propose a payment

tense
(زمان فعل)

stretch or force to the limit, tight

tension
(تنش)

action of stretching something tight, anxiety, feelings of hostility

terminal
(پایانه)

causing or ending in or approaching death, station

terminate
(خاتمه دادن)

stop, bring to an end or halt

terribly
(وحشتناک)

dreadfully, frightfully, to a great extent, very much

terrific
(فوق العاده)

causing extreme terror, very great, extraordinarily good

territory
(قلمرو)

large extent of land, organized portion of country

terror
(ترور)

extreme fear, violent dread, fright

testify
(گواهی دادن)

give testimony in a court of law, provide evidence for

testimony (شهادت) solemn declaration or affirmation, something that serves as evidence	**text** (متن) written words, book prepared for use in schools or colleges
textile (منسوجات) cloth, fabric	**theft** (سرقت) act of taking something from someone unlawfully, stealing
theme (موضوع) subject of conversation or discussion, topic, essay	**theoretical** (نظری) not practical or applied, hypothetical, of or based on theory
thereby (در نتیجه) thus, accordingly, by that means, because of that	**therefore** (از این رو) consequently, hence
thermometer (دماسنج) instrument for measuring temperature	**thigh** (ران) part of the leg between the hip and the knee
thirst (تشنگی) sensation of dryness in the throat	**thorough** (کامل) accurate or careful, complete
thoughtful (متفکر) considerate, having intellectual depth, giving close attention	**threaten** (تهدید) pose a threat to, present a danger to
threshold (آستانه) entrance, starting point for a new state or experience	**thrive** (شکوفا شدن) make steady progress, prosper, flourish
throat (گلو) part of neck in front of, passage to stomach and lung	**throng** (ازدحام) large group of people gathered or crowded closely together
thumb (شست) short, thick first digit of human hand	**tick** (تیک بزنید) emit recurring clicking sounds, do well or as designed

tide
(جزر و مد)
periodic rise and fall of the sea level

tighten
(سفت کردن)
draw tighter, straiten, make closer in any manner.

timber
(چوب)
wood, lumber, trees or wooded land considered as a source of wood

timely
(به موقع)
being or occurring in good time, sufficiently early, seasonable

title
(عنوان)
right or claim to possession, mark of rank, name of a book or film

toe
(انگشت پا)
one of digits of the foot, forepart of a foot or hoof

tolerate
(تحمل کردن)
endure, withstand, allow without prohibiting or opposing, permit

topic
(موضوع)
subject of a speech, essay, thesis, discussion, or conversation

torch
(مشعل)
large candle or lamp giving flaring flame, flashlight

torrent
(تورنت)
rushing stream, flood, heavy downpour

torture
(شکنجه)
extreme pain, anguish of body or mind

tough
(سخت است)
hard, difficult, feeling physical discomfort or pain, hard to bear

tow
(دوتایی)
draw or pull behind by a chain or line

towel
(حوله)
rectangular cloth or paper for drying or wiping

trace
(پی گیری)
follow, discover, make a mark or lines on a surface

tractor
(تراکتور)
a truck that has a cab but no body

tradition
(سنت)
thought or behavior followed from generation to generation, heritage

tragedy
(تراژدی)
disaster, event resulting in great loss and misfortune

trail
(دنباله)
path or track roughly through wild or hilly country, overland route

traitor
(خائن)
one who violates his allegiance and betrays his country

tramp
(با صدا راه رفتن)
travel or wander through, cleanse clothes in water

trample
(پایمال کردن)
destroy, step on

tranquil
(آرام)
free from disturbance, pacific

transform
(تبدیل)
change in outward structure or looks, convert

transit
(ترانزیت)
act of passing, passage through or over, line or route of passage

transition
(انتقال)
going from one state of action to another

transmission
(انتقال)
act of transmitting, automotive assembly of gears, sending of a signal

transmit
(انتقال، رساندن)
forward, send from one person or place to another

transparent
(شفاف)
easily detected, permitting light to pass through freely

transplant
(پیوند)
act of uprooting and moving a plant to a new location

transport
(حمل و نقل)
carry from one place to another, carry away, deport

trap
(دام)
catch, hold or catch as if in a hole

traverse
(عبور)
go through or across, often under difficult conditions

tread
(آج)
step on, mate with, place the foot

treason
(خیانت)
disloyalty, betrayal of trust or confidence

treatment
(رفتار)
handling, care that are intended to relieve illness or injury

treaty
(معاهده)
act of treating for the adjustment of differences, negotiation

tremendous
(عظیم)
huge, capable of making one tremble, terrible

trend
(روند)
popular taste, general direction in which something tends to move

trickle
(سرماخوردگی)
flow in drops, run or flow slowly, drip

trifle
(چیز جزیی)
a thing of very little value or importance

trigger
(ماشه)
cause something happen, set off

trim
(تر و تمیز کردن)
clip, cut down to the desired size or shape

triumph
(پیروزی)
victory, win, expressing great joy

trivial
(بدیهی)
unimportant, of little significance or value, ordinary, commonplace

tropical
(گرمسیری)
relating to region on either side of the equator, hot and humid

trumpet
(شیپور)
brass musical instrument with brilliant tone

tub
(وان)
a large open vessel for holding or storing liquids

tube
(لوله)
hollow cylindrical shape, underground railway

tumble
(فرو ریختن)
fall down, as if collapsing

tumult
(توفان)
noise, as made by a crowd, riot or uprising

tunnel
(تونل)
passageway through or under something, usually underground

turbulent
(آشفته)
characterized by unrest or disorder

tutor
(مدرس)
guide, give individual instruction

twig
(شاخه)
small branch or division of a branch

twist
(پیچ - پیچیدن)
turn in the opposite direction, form into a spiral shape

typhoon
(طوفان)
tropical cyclone occurring in the western pacific, violent whirlwind

typical
(معمول)
conforming to a type, representative

tyrant
(ستمگر)
absolute ruler, sovereign unrestrained by law or constitution

ultimate
(نهایی)
final, being the last or concluding, fundamental, elemental, extreme

ultimately (در نهايت) as final consequence, at last, in the end	**ultraviolet** (ماوراء بنفش) wave lengths shorter than light but longer than x rays
unanimous (مَتَّفق القَول) uniform, in complete agreement	**unconscious** (بيهوش) lacking awareness, senseless, unaware
uncover (برملا كردن) remove the cover from, expose, disclose	**underestimate** (دست كم گرفتن) make too low an estimate of the quantity, undervalue
undergo (تحت) experience, suffer, pass through	**underground** (زير زمين) under the level of the ground, buried
underline (تأكيد) mark a line below, as words, underscore.	**underneath** (در زير) under or below an object or a surface, lower down on the page
undertake (بعهده گرفتن) take on, embark on, assume	**undertaking** (تعهد) task or assignment undertaken, career
undo (خنثیسازی) release, cause the ruin or downfall of, cancel or reverse an action	**undue** (ناروا، بی مورد) not due, not yet owing, not just, proper, or legal, , excessive
uneasy (ناراحت) not easy, difficult, restless, disturbed by pain, anxiety	**unfair** (غير منصفانه) unjust, contrary to laws or conventions, especially in commerce
unfold (آشكار شدن) extend or stretch out to a greater or the full length, happen	**unfortunately** (متأسفانه) unluckily, by bad luck
uniform (لباس فرم) consistent, standardized, clothing of a particular group	**unique** (منحصر بفرد) without an equal, being the only one of its kind

unity (وحدت) cohesion, harmony, quality of being united into one	**universe** (کائنات) cosmos, everything that exists anywhere
unlikely (بعید) improbable, has little chance of being the case or coming about	**unload** (تخلیه) take something off a container
unsatisfactory (نامطلوب) not giving satisfaction, inadequate	**uphold** (حمایت) support, preserve, hold aloft, raise
upset (ناراحت) concerned by anxious uneasiness or trouble or grief	**urban** (شهری) metropolitan, of, relating to, or located in a city
urge (ترغیب) force in an indicated direction, stimulate, excite	**urgent** (فوری) pressing, compelling immediate action or attention
utility (ابزار) something useful, public service	**utilization** (استفاده) state of having been made use of, the act of using
utilize (استفاده) put into service, take advantage of	**utmost** (بیشترین) farthest point or extremity, most distant, extreme
utter (مطلقا) speak, express, send forth with the voice	**utterance** (گفتن) vocal expression, power of speaking, last or utmost extremity
vacancy (جای خالی) absence, emptiness	**vacant** (خالی) void of thought or knowledge, without an occupant or incumbent
vacation (تعطیلات) leisure time away from work, act of making something legally void	**vacuum** (خلاء) empty area or space, electrical home appliance that cleans by suction

vague
(مبهم)
imprecise, indistinct, not clearly expressed, inexplicit

valid
(معتبر)
logically convincing, sound, legally acceptable, well grounded

validity
(اعتبار)
quality of having legal force or effectiveness

valve
(شیر فلکه)
device or structure for controlling the flow of a fluid

vanish
(ناپدید شد)
disappear, pass out of sight, especially quickly, die out

variable
(متغیر)
factor, something that is likely to vary, changeable, inconstant

variant
(گونه)
varying in from, character, or the like, variable, different, diverse.

variation
(تغییر)
act of changing or altering

varied
(متنوع)
differed, diversified, various

variety
(تنوع)
diversity, quality or condition of being various or varied

various
(مختلف)
different, diverse, several, manifold, changeable, uncertain

vegetable
(سبزی)
any of numerous herbaceous plants to eat in meal

vein
(رگ)
blood vessel that carries blood

venture
(ریسک)
put at risk, adventure

verify
(تأیید کنید)
confirm, prove the truth of by presentation of evidence or testimony

verse
(آیه)
a piece of poetry

vertical
(عمودی)
upright in position or posture, oriented vertically

vessel
(کشتی)
craft, ship, container for liquids

veteran
(کهنه کار)
someone who has given long service

via
(از طریق)
by the way of

vibrate
(لرزش)
shake, quiver, move or swing from side to side regularly

vibration
(لرزش)
act of vibrating, a shaky motion

vicinity
(مجاورت، همسایگی)
state of being near in space or relationship, proximity

victorious
(پیروز)
successful, being the winner in a contest or struggle

vigorous
(نیرومند)
robust, strong, energetic, and active in mind or body

vine
(تاک)
weak-stemmed plant that derives support from climbing

violate
(نقَض)
treat in a violent manner, abuse, do violence to, disturb, interrupt

violent
(خشن)
turbulent, intensely vivid or loud, by violence or bloodshed

violin
(ویولن)
small instrument with four strings, played with a bow, a fiddle

virtually
(تَقریباً)
almost completely, practically, essentially

virtue
(تَقوا)
goodness, moral excellence, good quality

viscous
(چسبناک)
sticky, gluey, having high resistance to flow

vision
(چشم انداز)
ability to see, sight, vivid mental image

vivid
(واضح)
bright, lively, graphic, having striking color

vocation
(حرفه)
career, profession

vogue
(رواج)
popular fashion, current state or style of general acceptance and use

void
(خالی)
emptiness, containing nothing, clear or empty a place

volcano
(آتشفشان)
fissure in the earth's crust through which molten lava and gases erupt

volume
(جلد)
capacity, amount of space occupied by an object

voluntary
(داوطلبانه)
done or undertaken of one's own free will, unforced

volunteer (داوطلب) person who performs or offers to perform a service voluntarily	**voter** (رای دهنده) a citizen who has a legal right to vote
vowel (حرف صدادار) speech sound made with the vocal tract open	**vulnerable** (آسیب پذیر) susceptible to wounds, capable of being wounded or hurt
wagon (واگن) any of various kinds of wheeled vehicles drawn by a horse or tractor	**waist** (کمر) narrowing of the body between the ribs and hips
waive (چشم پوشی) give up temporarily, yield, give up voluntarily, defer	**wardrobe** (جا رختی) tall cabinet, closet, or small room built to hold clothes
warehouse (انبار) depot, storehouse for goods and merchandise	**warfare** (جنگ) military service, military life, contest carried on by enemies
warrant (حکم) guarantee, assurance by seller, authorization or certification	**warrior** (جنگجو) fighter, combatant, one who is engaged in or experienced in battle
weary (خسته) tired, exhausted, physically or mentally fatigued	**weave** (بافت) pattern or structure by weaving , knit, interlace
weaver (بافنده) craftsman who weaves cloth	**wedding** (عروسی) marriage ceremony, act of marrying, anniversary of a marriage
weld (جوش) unite closely or intimately, join together by heating	**welfare** (رفاه) benefit, something that aids health or happiness
whereas (در حالیکه) while on the contrary, while at the same time	**whereby** (به موجب آن) by which, by what, how

whilst (در حالی که) while, at the same time	**whirl** (گرداب) act of rotating or revolving rapidly, state of confusion, tumult
wholesaler (عمده فروش) someone who buys large quantities of goods and resells to merchants	**wholesome** (سالم) conducive to sound health or well-being, beneficial
width (عرض) measurement of the extent of something from side to side	**willow** (بید) trees having usually narrow leaves
winding (سیم پیچی) twisting or turning, spiral	**wisdom** (خرد) quality of being wise, knowledge , results of wise judgments
wit (بذله گویی) intellect, mental ability, natural ability to perceive and understand	**withdraw** (کنار کشیدن) remove from, pull back, break from gathering, retreat, depart
withdrawal (برداشت از حساب) secession, retreat or retirement	**wither** (پژمرده) shrivel, decay, lose freshness, vigor, or vitality, loss of moisture
withstand (مقاومت در برابر) stand up against, successfully resist, oppose with force or resolution	**witness** (شاهد) someone who sees an event and reports what happened, observe, watch
worldwide (در سراسر جهان) global, universal, throughout the world	**worst** (بدترین) be better than, defeat, gain the advantage over
wrap (بسته بندی کردن) enclose, arrange or fold as a cover or protection	**wreck** (خراب کردن) destruction, destroy, smash or break forcefully
wring (پیچیدن) twist, squeeze, compress, especially so as to extract liquid	**wrinkle** (چین و چروک) a minor difficulty, a slight depression in the smoothness of a surface

Made in the USA
Middletown, DE
29 July 2024

58243073R00071